William Gaddis

Twayne's United States Authors Series

Warren French, Editor

University of Wales, Swansea

TUSAS 546

WILLIAM GADDIS
Credit: Miriam Berkley

William Gaddis

by Steven Moore

Twayne Publishers
A Division of G. K. Hall & Co. • *Boston*

William Gaddis

Steven Moore

Copyright 1989 by G. K. Hall & Co.
All rights reserved.
Published by Twayne Publishers
A Division of G. K. Hall & Co.
70 Lincoln Street
Boston, Massachusetts 02111

Copyediting supervised by Barbara Sutton
Book production by Gabrielle B. McDonald
Book design by Barbara Anderson

Typeset in 11 pt. Garamond
by Compset, Inc., of Beverly, Massachusetts

Printed on permanent/durable acid-free paper
and bound in the United States of America

Library of Congress Cataloging-in-Publication Data

Moore, Steven, 1951–
    William Gaddis / by Steven Moore.
        p. cm.—(Twayne's United States authors series ; TUSAS 546)
    Bibliography: p.
    Includes index.
    ISBN 0-8057-7534-X
    1. Gaddis, William, 1922–   —Criticism and interpretation.
I. Title. II. Series.
PS3557.A28Z77   1989
813'.54—dc19   88-33371
                                                                               CIP

Contents

About the Author

Steven Moore was born in 1951 outside Los Angeles, educated mainly in Colorado and later at Rutgers University in New Jersey (Ph.D., 1988). He is the author/coeditor of two previous books on William Gaddis and also edited *The Vampire in Verse: An Anthology* (Dracula Press, 1985). He has published essays and reviews on a number of contemporary American writers and since 1987 has been an associate editor of the *Review of Contemporary Fiction*/Dalkey Archive Press.

Preface

William Gaddis is in the paradoxical position of being one of the most highly regarded yet least read novelists in contemporary American literature. Those who have taken the time to work their way through his massive, labyrinthine novels have usually emerged making extravagant claims on his behalf, but too many have been put off by the forbidding length and complexity of his work. His first novel, *The Recognitions* (1955), is nearly a thousand pages long and features a large cast, a dense plot, and a heavy cargo of erudition. His second, the National Book Award–winning *J R* (1975), is nearly as long, complex, and hugely cast and has the additional challenge of being presented almost entirely in dialogue without a single chapter break. Only Gaddis's third and most recent book, *Carpenter's Gothic* (1985), runs to conventional length, but even it packs into its 262 pages enough material for a novel twice its size. As daunting as these novels may appear, however, they are among the highest achievements of modern fiction and deserve far greater attention than they have hitherto received.

The Flemish painter, says Wyatt in *The Recognitions,* did not limit himself to a single perspective in a painting but instead took as many as he wanted. I follow his example in this book by taking not one but several critical approaches to Gaddis's novels. Thus chapter 2 on *The Recognitions* is a Jungian analysis of its mythic materials, while chapter 3 is an old-fashioned set of compare-and-contrast character analyses. Chapter 4 on *J R* is a set of mini-essays on such matters as style, intellectual background, the use of children as spokespeople, the Freudian implications of money, mechanization metaphors, and the plight of the artist, while chapter 5 studies the novel's principal allusions to Wagnerian opera, Victorian literature, and Greek philosophy. Chapter 6 is a genre study of *Carpenter's Gothic,* or more specifically, of Gaddis's adaptation of various genres within this novel. These chapters are preceded by an introductory chapter that skates on the thin ice of such topics as autobiography, influences, and intentions, and are followed by a conclusion that locates Gaddis in the various traditions of American literature he has both followed and enhanced.

Mr. Gaddis looked over a draft of the first chapter and kindly gave his permission to quote from his published and unpublished writings. Richard Scaramelli read each chapter as it was written and offered innumerable suggestions for improvement; I thank him for those and for his moral support, and also thank our mutual friend Clifford S. Mead for continuing to send me materials I might otherwise have missed. Barry Qualls of Rutgers also read the manuscript and made many valuable suggestions. David Markson and Charles Monaghan provided useful background materials. Thanks also go to Miriam Berkley for her photograph of Gaddis's "haggardly alert face" and for sharing the typescript of her interview with him; to Lucy Ferriss at Bard College for Gaddis's course description; to Grace Eckley for permission to publish a letter Gaddis wrote her; to my editors Liz Traynor and Warren French, the first for her patience, the second for his warm encouragement; and to Random House, Inc., for permission to reprint the concluding lines of "Wise Men in Their Bad Hours," from *Selected Poetry of Robinson Jeffers,* copyright 1924 and renewed 1952 by Robinson Jeffers.

Steven Moore

Chronology

1984   Inducted into the American Academy and Institute of
       Arts and Letters.

1985   *Carpenter's Gothic* published 22 July along with reissues
       of first two novels.

1986   *Carpenter's Gothic* published in England.

1987   Begins contributing more regularly to periodicals and
       works on a fourth novel.

Chapter One
A Vision of Order

The misjudgment of one generation is always a source of amazement to the next. It is hard to believe now that Melville was ignored by his generation of critics, that Samuel Butler was a literary pariah to his, and that Malcolm Cowley had to reintroduce Faulkner to his. William Gaddis's first novel, *The Recognitions,* was published in 1955, remaindered a few years later, and largely ignored for a generation. Only after the publication of his second novel, *J R,* in 1975 did critics begin to realize that *The Recognitions* pioneered (among other things) the black humor of the fifties and sixties and the Menippean satire of the seventies; only then was Gaddis recognized as "a presiding genius, as it turns out, of post-war American fiction."[1] Even though Gaddis's third novel, *Carpenter's Gothic* (1985), consolidated his place in the front rank of contemporary novelists, Gaddis remains one of the least read of major American writers. New critical studies of contemporary American fiction still appear that make no mention of his work, and a survey of any college's literature staff would probably reveal that many professors have not even heard of Gaddis, much less read him. Yet one professor who has, Frank D. McConnell, goes so far to say "that *The Recognitions* is the indispensable novel of the last thirty years in America, and that contemporary fiction makes no real sense without the presence of this strange, perverse, confusing, and ultimately sane book."[2]

This discrepancy can be accounted for in several ways. *The Recognitions,* for example, was cursed with inadequate reviews and an indifferent publisher who kept it only intermittently in print. The sheer size of *The Recognitions* and *J R* has scared off many, and although these and *Carpenter's Gothic* are now available in Penguin paperbacks, their reputation for difficulty intimidates many more. Nor has Gaddis made much effort to promote his work; until recently (and even then, grudgingly), Gaddis gave no interviews, avoided the literary limelight, and kept even interested critics at arm's length by insisting that the work must speak for itself.

The Man Inside

"I have generally shied from parading personal details partly for their being just that,"[3] he once explained, and perhaps partly for the same reason painter Wyatt Gwyon, the protagonist of *The Recognitions,* avoids showings of his work. Meeting him for the first time, the art critic Basil Valentine tells Wyatt:

—Seeing you now, you know, it's answered one of the questions I've had on my mind for some time. The first thing I saw, it was a small Dierick Bouts, I wondered then if you used a model when you worked.
—Well I . . .
—But now, it's quite obvious isn't it, Valentine went on, nodding at the picture between them. —Mirrors?
—Yes, yes of course, mirrors. He laughed, a constricted sound, and lit a cigarette.[4]

Gaddis too works from mirrors, drawing extensively on his own background for the characters and settings in his novels. Born in Manhattan in 1922, he was reared in Massapequa, Long Island, in the house that was the model for the Bast home in *J R.* Like the Basts, his mother's people were Quakers, though he himself was raised in a Calvinist tradition, as is Wyatt, who nonetheless "looks like a Kwa-ker" to one observer (585). Like Otto in *The Recognitions* and Jack Gibbs in *J R,* Gaddis grew up without his father, who divorced his mother when Gaddis was three. Haunting all three novels, in fact, is the spirit of a dead or absent father who leaves a ruinous state of affairs for his children to grapple with, a situation that can be extrapolated to include Gaddis's vision of a world abandoned by God *(deus absconditus)* and plunged into disorder.

His fifth through thirteenth years were spent at a boarding school in Berlin, Connecticut, which not only furnished Jack Gibbs with the bleak memories recalled in *J R* but also provided the unnamed setting for the New England chapters of *The Recognitions.* Returning to Long Island to attend Farmingdale High School, Gaddis contracted the illness that kept him out of World War II a few years later, much to his disappointment. Already enrolled at Harvard by that time, he stayed on and later edited the *Harvard Lampoon* until circumstances required him to leave in 1945 without a degree.

Moving to Horatio Street in Greenwich Village—the street on

which Wyatt lives while painting his forgeries—Gaddis worked as a
fact checker at the *New Yorker* for little over a year, a job he later
recalled as *"terribly* good training, a kind of post-graduate school for a
writer, checking everything, whether they were stories or profiles or
articles. I still feel this pressure of trying to make sure that I've got it
right. A lot of the complications of high finance and so forth in *J R*—
I tried very hard to get them all right. And it was very much that two
years at the *New Yorker.*"⁵ He quit the job to try his hand at commercial
short stories, without success, then set off in 1947 for five years of
wandering through Mexico and Central America, Europe (mostly Spain
and France), and North Africa. He worked on his first novel during
these travels, returning to America in 1952 to revise it through two
isolated winters. From Long Island he occasionally came into the city
to mingle in the Greenwich Village milieu so mercilessly re-created in
the middle section of *The Recognitions,* and eventually became acquainted with most of the emerging writers of the time.

   The Recognitions appeared in 1955 as the leading controversial literary
title on Harcourt, Brace's spring list (or so they treated it), but the
novel had little immediate success, as was the case with *Moby-Dick* a
century earlier. A few readers recognized its significance and provided
Gaddis with a cult following, but most reviewers were put off by this
gargantuan novel by an unknown writer. Looking back in 1975, John
Aldridge, an early champion, gave this explanation:

As is usually the case with abrasively original work, there had to be a certain
passage of time before an audience could begin to be educated to accept *The
Recognitions.* The problem was not simply that the novel was too long and
intricate or its vision of experience too outrageous, but that even the sophisticated reading public of the mid-Fifties was not yet accustomed to the kind
of fiction it represented. [. . .] The most authoritative mode in the serious
fiction of the Fifties was primarily realistic, and the novel of fabulation and
Black Humor—of which *The Recognitions* was later to be identified as a distinguished pioneering example—had not yet come into vogue. In fact, the writers who became the leaders of the Black Humor movement had either not
been heard from in 1955 or remained undiscovered. [. . .] Their work over
the past 20 years has created a context in which it is possible to recognize
Gaddis's novel as having helped inaugurate a whole new movement in American fiction. Rereading it with the knowledge of all that this movement has
taught us about modern experience and the opening of new possibilities for
the novel, one can see that *The Recognitions* occupies a strikingly unique and
primary place in contemporary literature.⁶

After it became apparent the novel was not going to supply him the kind of success he had envisioned, Gaddis began a series of jobs in industry that would later provide some raw material for his second novel. After working in publicity for a pharmaceutical firm, he wrote film scripts for the army and later speeches for corporate executives—as does Thomas Eigen in *J R,* who has likewise published an important but neglected novel. With the appearance in 1970 of "J.R. or the Boy Inside," which would later become the opening pages of his second novel, Gaddis broke his fifteen-year literary silence, and in the fall of 1975 *J R* was published to much stronger reviews than his first novel had received. Yet even though it won the National Book Award for the best fiction of the year, there are grounds, unfortunately, for Frederick Karl's complaint that *J R* remains "perhaps the great unread novel of the postwar era."[7]

Through the seventies Gaddis continued free-lance writing and performed brief teaching stints, usually in creative writing. At Bard College he developed a course on the theme of failure in American literature, a central theme in his own fiction and the subject of his brilliant essay "The Rush for Second Place" (1981), the best of his few nonfiction pieces. Meanwhile, critical commentary began forming around his two novels: essays began appearing with some regularity in scholarly journals, dissertations proliferated, all culminating in the summer of 1982 with the first book on his work, a special Gaddis issue of the *Review of Contemporary Fiction,* and a MacArthur Foundation fellowship (the so-called genius award). In 1984, a second book on his work appeared, Gaddis was elected to the American Academy and Institute of Arts and Letters, and he finished his third novel.

Like its predecessors, *Carpenter's Gothic* abounds in autobiographical elements. Not only does it take place in the same Victorian house Gaddis owns in Piermont, New York—where his papers are stored in the same garage-converted locked room that excites Liz's curiosity—but the house's absentee landlord, the geologist McCandless, offers yet another mirror image of Gaddis: "His face appeared drained, so did the hand he held out to her, drained of colour that might once have been a heavy tan[, . . .] his still, sinewed hands and his . . . hard, irregular features bearing the memory of distant suns, the cool, grey calm of his eyes belying . . . belying?"[8] Belying Gaddis, perhaps, for the second half of this quotation is Liz's fictionalization of McCandless's appearance, and she later takes the process one step further away from its original by completing her description from a book:

she seized the pencil to draw it heavily through his still, sinewed hands, hard irregular features, the cool disinterested calm of his eyes and a bare moment's pause bearing down with the pencil on his hands, disjointed, rust spotted, his crumbled features dulled and worn as the bill collector he might have been mistaken for, the desolate loss in his eyes belying, belying . . . The towel went to the floor in a heap and she was up naked, legs planted wide broached by scissors wielded murderously on the [television] screen where she dug past it for the rag of a book its cover gone, the first twenty odd pages gone in fact, so that it opened full on the line she sought, coming down with the pencil on belying, a sense that he was still a part of all that he could have been. (95)

The obvious lesson here is that we are dealing with fiction, not life, and that despite the encouraging fact that McCandless shares Gaddis's appearance, marital history, political outlook, speech habits, even his pets, he is no more to be strictly identified with his author than is Otto, Gibbs, or Eigen. "No," Gaddis has warned, "characters all draw on some contradictory level of their author's life,"[9] and sometimes even change in the course of composition. In a television interview with Malcolm Bradbury, Gaddis illustrated this point with reference to Thomas Eigen: "I started him out as being, sort of getting my own back, as it were. He starts out being quite a good fellow who has had bad luck, but as it went on he became very unpleasant, and finally by the end of the novel, he was thoroughly unpleasant, thoroughly, because this is the way he developed in the novel. I gave up identifying with him, and started to hold him at arm's length. But I saw this really was who the man was; he was not just a man who had had bad luck, but his embittered state had turned him into a really, not anybody you'd want to know."[10]

This autobiographical impulse can likewise be found in the work of a number of Gaddis's contemporaries, and his various self-portraits do have elements of Mailer's egotism, Kerouac's self-absorption, Roth's defensiveness, and Barth's playfulness. But the impulse probably owes more, in Gaddis's case, to the sense in some lines of Robert Browning's poetry that Gaddis once copied into a 1983 issue of *Conjunctions* that featured an interview with his friend William H. Gass: "This trade of mine—I don't know, can't be sure / But there was something in it, tricks and all! / Really, I want to light up my own mind." Perhaps the rest, as Eliot says, is not our business. Gaddis continues to live in and around New York City, travels widely, and is at work on a fourth novel.[11]

Influences

The nature and extent of Gaddis's reading has elicited an unusually large amount of speculation, especially by reviewers and critics eager to establish "influences" with which they can then damn or praise his work. Because of the allusions, quotations, and the encyclopedic range of knowledge displayed in the novels, especially in *The Recognitions*, Cynthia Ozick's front-page cry "Mr. Gaddis knows almost everything"[12] echoes critics who assume he has read everything. For example, Tony Tanner confidently states, "Clearly, Gaddis has read Joyce (what hasn't he read?),"[13] but Joyce is the most glaring example of an author whom Gaddis has not read, much less imitated. Similarly, Frederick Karl praises Gaddis's "extensive reading in and knowledge of religious literature, church fathers and historians, Latin works, church theologians, all sufficiently assimilated so that they can be regurgitated for parodic purposes,"[14] although nearly all of the religious references in *The Recognitions* can be traced to a half dozen rather mundane sources. Delmore Schwartz was closer to the mark when he wrote to Gaddis's friend and editor Catharine Carver, "he knows a lot more about sleeping pills than about the Church, despite the allusions."[15] This is not to denigrate Gaddis's undeniable learning: he is obviously an extremely well-read man who researches his books thoroughly, and these uncritical claims for his extensive knowledge are testimony to his artistry. Like most writers, Gaddis wears his influences most plainly on his sleeve in his first novel; with *J R* he clearly became his own man and "influences" all but disappear into the vast machinery of his work. But the nagging question of influences has been answered in so many misleading ways that a brief survey of Gaddis's reading—compiled from his books, letters, lectures, and conversation—seems warranted.

Gaddis majored in English literature at Harvard and remembers the program as solid and traditional: "we read Chaucer, we read Dryden and so forth, Elizabethan drama, Restoration comedy, all the things that a good education in that area gives you. And very little current. I mean, it was before the days of writing workshops, and discussing current novels, and so forth. It was much more . . . I can't call it 'classic' education, because that was much more Greek and Latin, but it was more old fashioned, which I'm delighted, I'm very glad of. I always have been very happy about that."[16]

Among others, he studied under Albert Guerard, attended F. O. Matthiessen's lectures on Greek drama, and was tutored in Chaucer by

Theodore Spencer. Gaddis looked at Spencer's edition of Joyce's *Stephen Hero* (1944) but was not impressed, and he did not look at much more of Joyce's work. Yet of all the alleged influences on Gaddis's work, Joyce has been named most often. The first academic essay on *The Recognitions* was a detailed demonstration of the novel's debt to *Ulysses,* "established in such minute detail," Gaddis later joked, "I was doubtful of my own firm recollection of never having read *Ulysses.*"[17] To this day the influence of Joyce is routinely assumed by many critics, despite several published denials by Gaddis. With justifiable impatience, he gave this emphatic answer to Joyce scholar Grace Eckley in 1975:

I appreciate your interest in *The Recognitions* & have to tell you I've about reached the end of the line on questions about what I did or didn't read of Joyce's 30 years ago. All I read of *Ulysses* was Molly Bloom at the end which was being circulated for salacious rather than literary merits; No I did not read *Finnegans Wake* though I think a phrase about "psychoanaloosing" one's self from it is in *The Recognitions;*[18] Yes I read some of *Dubliners* but don't recall how many & remember only a story called "Counterparts"; Yes I read a play called *Exiles* which at the time I found highly unsuccessful; Yes I believe I read *Portrait of an Artist* but also think I may not have finished it; No I did not read commentary on Joyce's work & absorb details without reading the original. I also read, & believe with a good deal more absorbtion, Eliot, Dostoevski, Forster, Rolfe, Waugh, why bother to go on, anyone seeking Joyce finds Joyce even if both Joyce & the victim found the item in Shakespear, read right past whole lines lifted bodily from Eliot &c, all of which will probably go on so long as Joyce remains an academic cottage industry.[19]

Eliot and Dostoyevski are the most significant names here; none of Gaddis's reviewers described *The Recognitions* as *The Waste Land* rewritten by Dostoyevski (with additional dialogue by Ronald Firbank), but that would be a more accurate description than the *Ulysses* parallel so many of them harped upon. Not only do Gaddis's novels contain dozens of "whole lines lifted bodily from Eliot," but *The Recognitions* can be read as an epic sermon using *The Waste Land* as its text. The novel employs the same techniques of reference, allusion, collage, multiple perspective, and contrasting voices; the same kinds of fire and water imagery drawn from religion and myth; and both call for the same kinds of artistic, moral, and religious sensibilities. *J R* is not as Eliotic as the first novel, yet it too contains several quotations from "The Love Song of J. Alfred Prufrock," "Hysteria," *The Waste Land,* and *Sweeney Agonistes,* all done in different voices. *Four Quartets,* so important to

the religious aura of *The Recognitions* that Gaddis at an early stage
planned to weave every one of its lines into his text, is conspicuous in
its absence in the profane world of *J R* and nearly invisible in the
despairing one of *Carpenter's Gothic*.

Among novelists, Dostoyevski's importance is paramount. "How are
we to write / The Russian novel in America / As long as life goes so
unterribly?" Robert Frost asked with uncharacteristic obtuseness in his
poem "New Hampshire," written about the time Gaddis was born.
Life proved terrible enough by the 1950s to produce in *The Recognitions*
the most "Russian" novel in American literature. Gaddis's love for
nineteenth-century Russian literature in general crops up in his novels,
his letters, and in his few lectures, where references are made to the
major works of Dostoyevski, Tolstoy (especially the plays), Gogol, Turgenev, Gorky, Goncharov, and Chekhov. Gaddis shares with these authors not only their metaphysical concerns and often bizarre sense of
humor, but their nationalistic impulses as well. William H. Gass reported a talk of Gaddis's in Lithuania where Gaddis insisted "he and
the earlier Russian writers had the same target, and that he was attempting to save his version of an acceptable country as they were
endeavoring to redeem theirs."[20] In each of his novels, moreover, Gaddis pursues what Edward Wasiolek has called "perhaps the most dis-
tinctive trait of Russian fiction, to trace out the extreme, but logically
possible, reaches of a human characteristic."[21]

Among western European writers, briefly, relevant works include
Sade's *Justine,* Goethe's *Faust,* Rilke's *Duino Elegies,* Rimbaud's *A Season
in Hell,* Broch's *Sleepwalkers,* Hesse's *Steppenwolf,* Silone's *And He Hid
Himself,* some Ibsen, and Dante. Kafka's *The Castle* is alluded to in
J R, and Gaddis once admitted that when he first read Kafka in his
early twenties he was so stunned by what Kafka could do that he "sat
down and wrote some very bad Kafka, though I thought of it as good
Kafka then."[22] He also read Gide's *Counterfeiters* when young, but
doubts it influenced his own novel about counterfeiters. He has never
read Robbe-Grillet (though parallels have been noted), nor Proust's
vast novel beyond its "overture," but read Montherlant's *Bachelors* and
apparently *The Girls* tetralogy. He keeps up with many middle European authors and, among Third World authors, has spoken highly of
Amos Tutuola's *The Palm-Wine Drinkard* and, in *Carpenter's Gothic,*
quotes V. S. Naipaul's *The Mimic Men.*

The range of relevant British writers is much greater, extending
from Langland's *Piers Plowman* and the medieval passion play *Harrow-*

ing of Hell through most of Shakespeare (*As You Like It* is his favorite) and other Elizabethan dramatists, Donne, Restoration and Augustan satirists, to a number of twentieth-century writers. Forster and Waugh, mentioned in the letter to Eckley, are discernible in Gaddis's mordant social criticism and use of foreign locales; he seems to have read and relished the bulk of these novelists' work. Rolfe's name is as surprising as it is little known, but in the unique writings of the self-styled Baron Corvo can be found anticipations of the virulent satire, haughty elitism, and outlandish erudition so prevalent in *The Recognitions*. A more obvious influence is the work of Ronald Firbank, whose unexampled novels were enjoying a revival when Gaddis was at work on his first novel. From these witty, outrageous novels Gaddis may have learned how to use elliptical dialogue—especially for effects usually achieved only in traditional exposition—and perhaps how to have campy fun at Catholicism's expense. (Gaddis may have learned from other masters of the novel in dialogue—especially early Waugh and late Henry Green—but Firbank's example is the most apparent.) Other British writers alluded to in Gaddis's writings include Charlotte Brontë (whose *Jane Eyre* made it into *Carpenter's Gothic* as a last minute substitute for *Lost Horizon,* which James Hilton's estate would not allow Gaddis to use), Butler's *The Way of All Flesh,* much Conrad, some Wilde and Kipling, Norman Douglas's *South Wind,* George Borrow's nonfiction, C. M. Doughty and T. E. Lawrence's classic books on Arabia, some Huxley and Maugham, much Robert Graves, and Sillitoe's *The Loneliness of the Long Distance Runner.* Among the poets, Browning, Tennyson, and Yeats are the most often quoted after Eliot.

Gaddis only recently read the British novel that most resembles *The Recognitions*—Malcolm Lowry's *Under the Volcano,* having earlier "found it coming both too close to home and too far from what I thought I was trying to do," he told David Markson.[23] But Lowry read Gaddis's novel at Markson's suggestion and, in a letter to Markson written shortly before his death, praised *The Recognitions* as "a veritable Katchenjunga, you know the mountain I mean anyhow, of a book, the ascent of some overhang of which can scarcely be made safely without the assistance, one feels, of both Tenzing and Aleister Crowley. [. . .] What I can say is that it is probably all you claim for it, a truly fabulous creation, a Super Byzantine Gazebo and secret missile of the soul and likewise extraordinarily funny: much funnier than Burton['s *Anatomy of Melancholy*] though Burton is a good parallel."

Despite his background in British and continental literature, however, Gaddis is first and foremost an American writer working with traditional American themes. Two in particular stand out: the first is the theme of failure, a theme so prevalent that it can be overlooked, he writes, "only by overlooking the main body of American literature and the novelists who have been struggling with the bitter truths of conflict and failure in American life."[24] His reading list at Bard consisted of such works as Bellamy's *Looking Backward,* Dreiser's *Sister Carrie* and *An American Tragedy,* Sinclair's *The Jungle,* Lewis's *Babbitt,* Frost's "Provide, Provide," Miller's *Death of a Salesman,* Salinger's *The Catcher in the Rye,* and more recent novels such as Joan Didion's *Play It As It Lays,* Sue Kaufman's *Diary of a Mad Housewife,* and Frederick Exley's *A Fan's Notes.* (Among the nonfiction he used are James's *Pragmatism,* Carnegie's *How to Win Friends and Influence People,* Hofstadter's *Social Darwinism in American Thought,* Riesman's *The Lonely Crowd,* and John Holt's *How Children Fail.*) The theme of failure is one of the two most important themes in *J R* (both spelled out in the novel's final paragraph by J R himself as "success and like free enterprise") and is a thematic common denominator for all of Gaddis's work.

The vehicle Gaddis uses to convey this theme aligns him with another American literary tradition, what D. H. Lawrence facetiously calls "the great American grouch,"[25] "Much of our fiction," Gaddis declared in a 1986 address, "going back well over a century, has been increasingly fueled by outrage or, at the least, by indignation. Curiously enough, this is often coupled with and even springs from the writer's perennially naive notion that through calling attention to inequalities and abuses, hypocrisies and patent frauds, self deceiving attitudes and self defeating policies, these will be promptly corrected by a grateful public; but the state is the public's fiction, and gratitude is not its most prominent attribute."[26] Satire intended to be as edifying as it is caustic is an American staple going back to the first big novel in our literature, Brackenridge's *Modern Chivalry.* Gaddis probably doesn't know this work, but he does know the work of a good many later moral satirists: Hawthorne (he's read *The Scarlet Letter* and *The Blithedale Romance,* but not *A Marble Faun,* as has been suggested), Melville (*Moby-Dick,* "Bartleby the Scrivener," and *Billy Budd,* but he never finished *The Confidence-Man*), some Emerson (mostly at second hand), Thoreau's *Walden,* Crane's *Maggie,* a good deal of Mark Twain (both fiction and nonfiction), Nathanael West, Cummings (especially *1 × 1*), and, among his contemporaries, Heller, early Burroughs, and later Elkin.

Other American writers, not necessarily Lawrence's grouches, that Gaddis has read include Djuna Barnes (her stories as well as *Nightwood*), Faulkner (only *The Sound and the Fury* and a few stories, he confesses), and like every writer of his generation, Hemingway. He seems to have little interest in the works of those contemporary novelists with whom he is most often associated: John Barth, Robert Coover, Don DeLillo, John Hawkes, Joseph McElroy, Thomas Pynchon, Gilbert Sorrentino, and Alexander Theroux—all of whom apparently know his work. Instead, he seems to prefer more traditional works over the kind of novels he himself writes—perhaps because he considers his work more traditional than his critics do. He never finished either *Lolita* or *The Sot-Weed Factor* (both on stylistic grounds) but alludes to Capote's and Styron's first novels in his work, and he has recommended the work of such novelists as Joy Williams (specifically *State of Grace*) and James Salter. Saul Bellow's novels are apparently old favorites, and *More Die of Heartbreak* elicited from Gaddis his first book review since his *Lampoon* days. In general he seems more likely to pick up a novel like Jay McInerney's *Bright Lights, Big City* (which he found "very funny") than novels as challenging as his own, a common tendency among many novelists. But to conclude the question of influences, it is worth quoting Gaddis's response to the query whether he thought Pynchon's work might have been influenced by his own: "I haven't read Pynchon enough to have an opinion either of his work or whether it might have been 'influenced' (perilous word) by mine, though I've understood he feels not & who's to know if he'd ever read mine before V? Always a dangerous course."[27]

Intentions

The question of intentions is as dangerous a course to pursue as that of influences, but Gaddis's intentions have likewise been too often misjudged to leave them unexamined. In one of his essays Edward Hoagland suggests "writers can be categorized by many criteria, one of which is whether they prefer subject matter that they rejoice in or subject matter they deplore and wish to savage with ironies." Gaddis clearly belongs in the second camp, to the tradition of vitriolic satire fueled by moral indignation that goes back through the American writers named earlier to the great Augustan satirists of the eighteenth century, back through Voltaire, Ben Jonson, and the bitterly satirical Shakespeare of *Troilus and Cressida* and *Timon of Athens* (even *King Lear*), back finally to such classical satirists as Juvenal and Persius. Yet charges of nihilism and pessimism have dogged Gaddis from his earliest novel by those who feel his work is not based "on any but a narrow and jaundiced view, a projection of private discontent."[28] Such narrow and jaundiced views have been aired by those apparently unaware that satire is primarily a constructive, rather than destructive, artistic strategy, one that has as its quixotic goal the rejuvenation of society, not its ruin. Pope, for example, felt the satirist had a moral obligation to expose the faults of his society so that the necessary corrections could be made, and the same idealistic motivation spurred the Russian novelists Gaddis admires. Gaddis belongs to the company of "salutory assassins," as Gilbert Sorrentino puts it,[29] and all three of his novels can be read, in one sense at least, as crusades: in *The Recognitions,* against fraudulence and fakery at all levels (artistic, religious, intellectual, moral, political, etc.); in *J R,* against the abuses of capitalism, new-fangled pedagogy, and the farcical notion of corporate "democracy"; and in *Carpenter's Gothic,* against fundamentalism, sensationalist journalism, and every form of stupidity.

Like all satirists, Gaddis relies on humor to achieve his goals, encouraging the reader to laugh away the pretensions of all those he holds up to ridicule. The comic element in Gaddis's work, however, has been consistently underrated. Instead, undue weight has been placed on Gaddis's alleged negativity, much to the novels' disadvantage. He once addressed this charge in an interview with an answer that deserves to be quoted in full; asked if he considered his novels "apocalyptic," Gaddis replied:

You mean looking to a bad end? I don't know. A couple of reviews said about *J R* that everything in it is so negative, so bad, the artist is devoured by the business community, but I didn't see it that way at all, I saw it in a much more positive light. In both books this community does very much represent reality, the life which is going on, what one has to deal with. This is the outer demand, while what the artist does is from the inner demand. So that collision of the outer and inner demand is what it's all about. Many people have no inner demand, like J R. He is eleven years old, he is undeveloped, he has got nothing inside. The only values he knows are the ones he sees around him, which are: get ahead, succeed, make money, and so on. At the end, even though he has been put out of business, destroyed, he is still ready to go again and is looking for some new way to do it. He hasn't learned anything.[30] Whereas Bast, the composer, who at the beginning has these fantasies of composing a grand opera at twenty, then, colliding with reality, with the material—success—junk aspect of America, sees that he has to modify his demands. He spends 700 pages colliding with this world, and his ambitions go from a grand opera to a cantata, then he takes out the voices so he can write a suite, and finally there he is trying to write a solo piece for cello. But as he says at the end, "I've been making other people's mistakes, now I'm going to make my own mistakes." So he has in a way been purified, he has gone through the purgatory of material craziness, and now he says: "I've had it, now I'm going to do what I want to do!" That to me isn't a negative message at all. If you get that one positive thread it is all one can hope for, because the world isn't that friendly a place, really.

In *The Recognitions* you have a similar theme. When Wyatt starts out he is not a genius, but he is a very talented painter. But he has had a bad start with the critics and, disappointed, he turns to forgery, which is to say involvement with the material—money—junk world. But he comes out and at the end he is ready to start again. That is not negative at all. We live in a world of negative forces, but the message in both books is for me a very positive one. This eludes many readers who say that they've never read anything so depressing in their lives. Well, it's enough to look around: bad things are there, you know. People ask, why don't I write nice books about happy people. But what do you say about happy people?[31]

Only with *Carpenter's Gothic* do the charges of pessimism have some validity. A positive message is conspicuously absent here, even though (to quote again from Aldridge) Gaddis's "awareness of what is human and sensible is always present behind his depiction of how far we have fallen from humanity and sense."[32] Asked shortly after the publication of this novel, "If your work could have a positive social/political effect, what would you want it to be?" Gaddis answered, "Obviously quite the opposite to what the work portrays."[33] But Gaddis's own outlook seems identical to that of McCandless, who reads his fate in a book he takes down from his shelf (Naipaul's *Mimic Men*): "*A man, I suppose, fights only when he hopes, when he has a vision of order, when he feels strongly there is some connexion between the earth on which he walks and himself. But there was my vision of a disorder which it was beyond any one man to put right*" (150). A vision of order apparently sustained Gaddis through his first two catalogs of disorder, but *Carpenter's Gothic* projects a vision of disorder as bleak as Pope's at the end of his *Dunciad,* one that seems to proceed, as the narrator of Melville's "Bartleby the Scrivener" puts it, "from a certain hopelessness of remedying excessive and organic ill."

Together, Gaddis's three novels constitute one of the most searching critiques of "what America is all about," as a character in *J R* would say. Gaddis, like Hawthorne and Melville before him, is the leading modern exemplar in American literature of what Leslie Fiedler would call a "tragic Humanist," a writer "whose duty is to say 'Nay!', to deny the easy affirmations by which most men live, and to expose the blackness of life most men try deliberately to ignore. For tragic Humanists, it is the function of art not to console or sustain, much less to entertain, but to *disturb* by telling a truth which is always unwelcome."[34] The sentiment is even more forcibly expressed by Gaddis's most recent protagonist/spokesman, the learned Judge Crease, who insists "the artist comes among us not as the bearer of *idées reçus* embracing art as decoration or of the comfort of churchly beliefs enshrined in greeting-card sentiments but rather in the aesthetic equivalent of one who comes on earth 'not to send peace, but a sword.'"[35]

Chapter Two

The Recognitions: Myth, Magic, and Metaphor

The length of three or four average novels, *The Recognitions* is many novels in one: a social satire, a pilgrim's progress, an anatomy of forgery, both a bildungsroman and kunstlerroman—not to mention a roman à clef—a philosophical romance, even a mystery story. Similarly, it is narrated from not one but several points of view and in as many styles. Wyatt could be speaking for Gaddis when he boasts of his latest forgery, "There isn't any single perspective, like the camera eye, the one we all look through now and call it realism, there . . . I take five or six or ten . . . the Flemish painter took twenty perspectives if he wished, and even in a small painting you can't include it all in your single vision, your one miserable pair of eyes" (251). The first-time reader of *The Recognitions* faces a similar challenge. Ranging across three continents and three decades, evoking four thousand years of cultural history, speaking half a dozen languages, and drawing upon fields of reference as diverse as alchemy, witchcraft, art history, mummification, medical history, hagiography, mythology, anthropology, astronomy, and metaphysics, *The Recognitions* threatens to overwhelm the hapless reader, who may be tempted to cry out with Wyatt, "But the discipline, the detail, it's just . . . sometimes the accumulation is too much to bear" (114).

"How ambitious you are!" his wife Esther responds, and it was Gaddis's ambition in this first novel to do no less than to excavate the very foundations of Western civilization, to expose to the harsh light of satire the origins of its religions, social structures, epistemologies, sexual ideologies, and its art forms. To do so, he created a protagonist whose difficulty assimilating his cultural/religious heritage and achieving a state of psychic wholeness would parallel the rocky road civilization itself has traveled toward that illusory goal. Ontogeny recapitulates phylogeny, and in Wyatt Gwyon's indecisions and difficulties we have a microcosm of the macrocosmic conflicts throughout history between patriarchy and matriarchy, God and Mammon, religion and the occult, the demands of the community and the imperatives of the self.

"The most sensitive individual, although not the most normal," Stephen Spender writes of Lowry's Consul, "may provide the most representative expression of a breakdown which affects other people on levels of which they may be scarcely conscious."[1] The breakdown in question, in *The Recognitions* as in *Under the Volcano,* is that of values, morals, standards. Gaddis's novel is primarily an account of personal integration amid this collective disintegration, of an individual finding himself in a society rapidly losing itself. In stark contrast to the dozens of other characters in *The Recognitions* who are indifferent to (when not the cause of) any breakdown in values, Wyatt is tortured by personal and ethical concerns that strike others as chimerical. "The boundaries between good and evil must be defined again," Esther taunts him, "they must be reestablished, that's what a man must do today, isn't it?" But Wyatt insists, "this moral action, it isn't just talk and . . . words, morality isn't just theory and ideas, that the only way to reality is this moral sense" (590–91).

Wyatt's pursuit of "reality" is conducted primarily on a metaphysical plane. All religions and occult traditions have at their base a belief in another, higher reality that transcends sensory reality, and Wyatt—like every true mystic, alchemist, and magician before him—searches for a window on that transcendent state where suddenly "everything [is] freed into one recognition, really freed into the reality that we never see" (92). Traditionally, this other reality (which "you can't see freely very often, hardly ever, maybe seven times in a life") has been literalized into such forms as a supercelestial heaven or a subterranean hell. But Wyatt is as convinced as Melville's Ahab that all visible objects are but as pasteboard masks, and the novel dramatizes his progress through institutionalized religion and the jejune theatricality of the occult, past the realms conquered and codified by overconfident scientists, to the timeless state beyond the reach of those who would make of God a science, or of science a god. This ineffable state resists description and accounts to some extent for the vagueness of Wyatt's final appearances and cryptic utterances; as Kafka told Max Brod, "You can't write salvation, only live it."[2]

This needs to be stated at the outset in order to make sense of the novel's complex matrix of allusions, references, iconography, and iterative imagery. For even though the novel addresses timely questions regarding the artist's place in the modern world—the one aspect of *The Recognitions* that has attracted the most critical attention—at its widest perimeters the novel is an encyclopedic survey of the varieties of religious experience. In one sense, all of the novel's major characters can be grouped into those "having, or about to have, or at the very least valiantly fighting off, a religious experience" (900), with the majority falling into the third category. Religious and mythic parallels and parodies, from the sublime to the blasphemous, abound in the novel. Not only does *The Recognitions* make extensive use of the primary colors of mythology's palette—sun and moon imagery, the infernal descent, death and rebirth motifs—but Wyatt's symbolic voyage from spiritual darkness to enlightenment follows (by way of quotation and allusion) in the wakes of such metaphysical wanderers as Odysseus, the Flying Dutchman, Faust, and Peer Gynt. Some indication of the scope of Gaddis's preoccupation with religion in this novel is given by the range of sources he used in composition: from the third-century theological romance attributed to Saint Clement from which *The Recognitions* takes its name, to the *Apocryphal New Testament,* Foxe's *Book of Martyrs,* Lethaby's *Architecture, Mysticism and Myth,* Frazer's *Golden Bough,* Phythian-Adams's *Mithraism,* Lang's *Magic and Religion,* Kramer and Sprenger's *Malleus Maleficarum,* Conybeare's *Magic, Myth, and Morals,* Marsh's *Mediæval and Modern Saints and Miracles,* the *Pilgrim Hymnal,* Summers's *Physical Phenomena of Mysticism,* Graves's *White Goddess,* and Edgar Saltus's survey of atheism, *The Anatomy of Negation.* In addition, there are more than a hundred citations from the Bible as well as references to almost every major religious and occult tradition, from the Egyptian *Book of the Dead* and Druidic practices to the writings of the early Church fathers, the Koran, legends of Krishna and the Buddha, Gnostic speculations, Saint Ignatius's *Spiritual Exercises,* hermetic alchemy, a calendar's worth of saints' lives, witchcraft manuals, Mithraic worship, Fortean hypotheses, magic numbers, Zuñi prayer sticks, excommunication rites (both Catholic and Jewish), even a Satanic invocation.[3]

All this led some reviewers to complain that the novel was "shrouded in mysticism" and filled with "pagan mumbo-jumbo."[4] But Gaddis is not merely indulging in arcane name-dropping; like art, religion is subject to decay and counterfeit, and Wyatt's obsession with authentic art is inextricably bound up with his obsession with authentic religious experience. In both realms, the genuine must be distinguished from the fake. Institutional religion receives little serious consideration in the novel, dismissed out of hand as an amateurish forgery or a poorly printed reproduction. Esme tells Otto that Wyatt once said "that saints were counterfeits of Christ, and that Christ was a counterfeit of God" (483), and most conventional forms of religion are ridiculed mercilessly in the novel. (Here, of course, Gaddis parts ways with Eliot, whose preoccupation with religion he otherwise shares.) Instead Wyatt finds in myth, magic, and mysticism a more authentic religious tradition, "religious that is in the sense of devotion, adoration, celebration of deity, before religion became confused with systems of ethics and morality, to become a sore affliction upon the very things it had once exalted" (311)—an attitude closer to the Pound of the later *Cantos* than to Eliot.

But the novel does not merely advocate a retreat from rational religion to irrational mysticism, or dropping the rosary to pick up a Buddhist prayer wheel. *The Recognitions* does have its supernatural moments, but its immense network of references to myth, religion, and the occult is deployed chiefly for psychological purposes. Carl Jung found in such spiritual traditions the validation needed for his theories of the process of individuation, and Gaddis's documented reliance on Jung's *Integration of the Personality*—a psychological commentary on alchemical symbolism—allows the reader to interpret Wyatt's "wild conflict" (247) in terms of the quest for psychic wholeness that Jung insists is at the heart of all mystical traditions. With Jung supplying the Ariadne's thread, readers can make their way through Gaddis's labyrinth of magic and myth with results that are as surprising as they are enlightening, perhaps even allowing *The Recognitions* itself to function as a heuristic, symbolic text in the tradition of alchemical tracts, and allowing Gaddis to succeed Melville as an "heir to the protestant tradition of New England, parodying with astonishing provincial vigour the old emblematic discourses of a Cotton Mather or Jonathan Edwards."[5]

Gaddis accomplishes this by narrating Wyatt's career on two parallel planes, the realistic and the mythic. The realistic concerns "a lonely little boy, getting upset over silly people" (118). Losing his mother at an early age, Wyatt is reared by a dour Calvinist aunt who discourages his talent for drawing in favor of a career in the ministry. Wyatt dutifully pursues the latter while secretly practicing the former, and after a year at divinity school sneaks off to Europe to study painting. Indifferent to the prevailing fashions in the art world of the 1930s, Wyatt works in the tradition of the Flemish painters of the late Middle Ages and allows an unsettling encounter with a corrupt art critic to discourage him from continuing his art. Drifting into a sterile marriage and a dull draftsman's job, Wyatt lets his artistic talents go to waste until Recktall Brown, discovering him in the depths of despair, tempts him away to forge Flemish paintings that his associate, Basil Valentine, will authenticate in the art journals—with all three enjoying the profits. Increasingly prey to guilt and thoughts of damnation, however, Wyatt later decides to forsake forgery and resume his studies for the ministry—a desperate act that fails when he returns home to find his father deranged. He extricates himself from his counterfeiting ring only after witnessing Brown's death and causing Valentine's (or so he thinks), after which he flees to Spain, where his mother is buried. Drifting through Spain and North Africa, he winds up at a monastery in Estremadura where he is finally able to free himself from the feelings of guilt, loneliness, and depression that had been accumulating since childhood. Whether he resumes his art or simply returns to his Spanish lover to raise their child are possibilities suggested but not confirmed as Wyatt, now called Stephen (as his mother first intended), resumes his journey, with the monastery bells ringing him on.

On the mythic plane, however, Wyatt's career adapts several models: he is an adept of hermetic alchemy, a Faust figure, a modern saint, the priest in the ancient cult–ritual of the White Goddess and her Son, the Wandering Jew/Flying Dutchman archetype, a near-victim in the sacrifical killing of the royal son, a Christ figure, Dante and Orpheus in the underworld, even the New Year Robin out to kill his father the Wren. In this respect, Gaddis does indeed resemble Joyce: by "manipulating a continuous parallel between contemporaneity and antiquity," Eliot felt Joyce had found "a way of controlling, of ordering, of giving a shape and a significance to the immense panorama of futility and anarchy which is contemporary history."[6] Gaddis pursues the same mythical method with equally intriguing results.

Masks and Mirrors

"Even Camilla had enjoyed masquerades," *The Recognitions* begins, "of the safe sort where the mask may be dropped at that critical moment it presumes itself as reality." But Gaddis is chiefly concerned with masquerades of the dangerous sort, where the mask has presumed itself as reality for so long that "reality," as Nabokov remarked, requires apologetic quotes. "It's like a masquerade isn't it," Herschel exclaims during the novel's first party scene; "I feel so naked, don't you? among all these frightfully masked people. Remember? de Maupassant, Guy de Maupassant of course, writing to that Russian girl, 'I mask myself among masked people'" (177). Herschel, however, is one of the few in the novel who can still recognize a mask when he sees one; the rest have grown so used to theirs that only an accidental glimpse in the mirror can recall them to themselves.

Masks and mirrors dominate the novel's iconography and carry the psychological values Jung assigned to them in *The Integration of the Personality*: "The man who looks into the mirror of the waters does, indeed, see his own face first of all. Whoever goes to himself risks a confrontation with himself. The mirror does not flatter, it faithfully shows whatever looks into it; namely, the face we never show to the world because we cover it with the *persona,* the mask of the actor. But the mirror lies behind the mask and shows the true face."[7] Wyatt, "that most dubious mirror-gazer of our acquaintance," is shown throughout the novel troubled by "the intimacies of catoptric communion" (673), avoiding the confrontation with himself Jung warns of. For others merely a confirmation of what they want to see, the mirror for Wyatt shows that authentic self he hasn't the strength to become, partially because of unresolved familial conflicts. "They are mirrors with terrible memories," Esme says of the ones in Wyatt's studio, "and they know, they *know,* and they tell him these terrible things and then they trap him" (221).

The most terrible things they tell him are that he has dishonored his mother and wants to kill his father. Wyatt is painfully aware of the first charge, and admits as much; speaking of Camilla's face in his forged *Stabat Mater,* Wyatt agrees with Valentine's interpretation: "Yes, the reproach! That's it, you understand?" (548). But the Oedipal conflict emerges only with close attention to the novel's avian symbolism, submerged in the text just as the conflict is submerged in Wyatt's unconscious. Gaddis learned from Robert Graves that "in British folklore, the Robin Red Breast as the Spirit of the New Year sets out with a birch-rod to kill his predecessor the Gold Crest Wren, the Spirit of the Old Year, whom he finds hiding in an ivy bush. [. . .] The robin is said to 'murder its father,' which accounts for its red breast."[8] Elsewhere, Graves identifies the Welsh Arianrhod (one of his White Goddesses) as "the mother of the usual Divine Fish-Child Dylan who, after killing the usual Wren (as the New Year Robin does on St. Stephen's Day) becomes Llew Llaw Gyffes," a Welsh hero with whom Wyatt associates himself (545). "The child Llew Llaw's exact aim was praised by his mother Arianrhod because as the New Year Robin, *alias* Belin, he transfixed his father the Wren, *alias* Bran to whom the wren was sacred, 'between the sinew and the bone' of his leg" in the manner of the Roman ritual of crucifixion.[9]

Wyatt is associated with the robin both via Llew Llaw and by way of his first work of art, the crude drawing of a robin so severely criticized by his Aunt May. The young Wyatt had killed a wren not on Saint Stephen's Day—though his use of a stone recalls the stoning of the proto-martyr, after whom Wyatt was intended to be named—but, significantly, on his mother's birthday (32). Too guilty at the time to confess the "murder," he blurts it out during his illness a few years later, to which his befuddled father responds with anthropological data from Frazer's *Golden Bough* (47), indicating he is clearly aware of the symbolic implications of his son's patricidal act. When Wyatt returns to his father in II.3 a few days before Christmas, the sight of a wren reminds him of his earlier transgression:

—I'll go out like the early Christian missionaries did at Christmas, to hunt down the wren and kill him, yes, when the wren was king, do you remember, you told me . . . When the wren was king, he repeated, getting his breath again, —at Christmas.

The wren had flown, as he turned from the window and approached with burning green eyes fixed on Gwyon. —King, yes, he repeated —when the king was slain and eaten, there's sacrament. There's sacrament. (430)

Wyatt's eyes had burned green at his first confession of killing the wren as a child (47), and the repetition of this sign of anger during his return (his second coming, as the servant Janet interprets it) follows Wyatt's ominous quotation of Matthew 10:21: "'and the children shall rise up against their parents, and cause them to be put to death'" (430). The anger directed at his father apparently springs from an unarticulated suspicion on Wyatt's part that his father was somehow responsible for his mother's death. All the young boy knew was that his father left with his mother but returned alone, and although the older Wyatt has learned the story of "the Spanish affair" (as his father calls it), the suspicion joins the other terrible things in the mirror.

Wyatt is also acting in self-defense. Rev. Gwyon broods over the chapter "The Sacrifice of the King's Son" in Frazer's *Golden Bough* (23), and Aunt May relentlessly indoctrinates Wyatt with a religion that centers on a father's deliberate sacrifice of his only begotten son. (The father's threat is symbolized by the straight-edged razor Wyatt takes from his father when he leaves for Europe; Esther recognizes it as a castrating symbol [90], and Anselm will later steal it for that exact purpose.) Wyatt's unconscious fears of death and/or castration at his father's hands surface for the last time when the Reverend Gwyon threatens to initiate him into the priesthood of Mithras, to whom the deranged minister is now devoted: "—Yes, at my hands, Gwyon said looking at him steadily, —you must die at the hands of the Pater Patratus, like all initiates" (432). Wyatt flees, but not without incurring additional guilt. Telling Valentine afterward of his trip home, Wyatt says, "I fell in the snow, killing wrens" (545); and by abandoning his deranged father Wyatt can be held indirectly responsible for the Reverend Gwyon's confinement and eventual crucifixion in II.9, just as Llew Llaw the robin symbolically crucified his father the wren.

The recurring references to the robin/wren conflict, to the killing of the king ("My father was a king," Wyatt tells Ludy at the end of the novel [892]), to the various myths of "the god killed, eaten, and resurrected" (536), to Wyatt's use of his father's face in his early Memling imitation of *The Flaying of the Unjust Judge,* and to the significant juxtaposition of symbolically killing his father on his mother's birthday— all point to a classic case of the Oedipus complex. By finally "eating" his father in III.5—his father's ashes have been mistakenly baked into the monastery's bread—-the sacrifical act is complete, and by allowing his father's painted face to drop on the ground unheeded (896), the conflict is resolved, the terrible voices from the mirror silenced at last.

Frazer follows his account of mirror superstitions (on which Gaddis drew) with similar superstitions surrounding portraits, which "are often believed to contain the soul of the person portrayed."[10] Most of the novel's major characters have their likenesses, if not their souls, captured on canvas. The Reverend Gwyon, as mentioned earlier, is flayed as the unjust judge in Wyatt's apprentice painting; Esther resembles "the portrait of a woman with large bones in her face but an unprominent nose" that her husband restores (88); Recktall Brown's ludicrous portrait is subjected to repeated ridicule; Anselm and Stanley resemble Kollwitz's print of two prisoners listening to music (524); Esme not only "looks like she thinks she *is* a painting. Like an oil you're not supposed to get too close to" (147) but models as the Virgin Mary in Wyatt's forgeries, with Wyatt taking the role of Christ crucified, as the Son mourned over by the Mother.

"Such pictures seem to have, for the patient, a psychological magic," Jung writes of a patient who likewise used painting as a means of attaining individuation. "Because pictorial expression fixes certain unconscious contents and draws others around it, he can work magic by this means, but only upon himself."[11] Wyatt's conscious, aesthetic conflicts with art have been treated elsewhere in Gaddis criticism,[12] but to comprehend his unconscious conflicts further, and the importance of his mother's appearances in her son's paintings, another pattern of mythic imagery must be introduced.

A Fluctuating Between Sun and Moon

In choosing to open the novel with Camilla's funeral, Gaddis draws attention to the character who makes the fewest appearances in the novel but nevertheless exerts the strongest influence on Wyatt: his mother. In fact, her only appearance in the temporal progression of the novel (thus excluding the flashbacks on pages 14 and 52) is as a wraith, appearing before three-year-old Wyatt at the moment of her death (20). The ability to see the ghost of one's mother, says Aniela Jaffé in her Jungian study *Apparitions and Precognition,* "indicate[s] an intensified unconscious, or a relatively easy and rapid lowering of the threshold of consciousness," and "points to a close relation with the unconscious, that is, a rootedness in the instinctual life," for "we must not forget that the 'mother' is a long established symbol for the unconscious."[13] Wyatt can see her, but Camilla vanishes upon Aunt May's entrance (just as the robin flees before her [40]), that is, before that which denies the unconscious, the instinctual, the emotional, and of course the irrational, thereby setting into motion a dichotomy active throughout the novel: the opposition between the unconscious and conscious, mother and father, instinct and intellect, emotion and rationality, night and day, paganism and Christianity, and so on. Warped by Aunt May's influence and only confused by Rev. Gwyon's, Wyatt will thereafter vacillate between two extremes represented by father and mother, like Stevens's Crispin voyaging "between two elements, / A fluctuating between sun and moon,"[14] until he learns that one extreme is not to be privileged over the other, but that the best qualities of each are to be integrated within.

This skeletal psychological program obviously needs fleshing out. The necessity of integrating the conscious and unconscious is not a

modern discovery but is rather of ancient provenance with a rich and
exotic history. It is at the heart of such unusual disciplines as alchemy,
witchcraft, Gnosticism, "true" poetry (as Robert Graves defines it in
The White Goddess), and other assorted heresies, all of which can be
found in the crowded first chapter of Gaddis's novel. Before the existence of the unconscious was posited by modern psychologists, its function was expressed in other terms by those who realized there is more
to perception than what ordinary daylight consciousness allows. Most
Platonic and oriental philosophies, all occult traditions, and the mystical branches of institutional religions speak of this alternative consciousness, and countless are the ways adepts have sought to tap its
unique powers. The most universal symbols for these two modes of
consciousness have been the sun and the moon; associated with the sun
are the so-called masculine traits of rationality, intellectualism, order,
separation, logic, etc.; the opposing "feminine" traits belong to the
moon: intuition, emotions, tenderness, harmony, and so forth. It has
become common, therefore, to speak of the opposition of solar consciousness to lunar consciousness: most intellectual activities and institutional religions employ solar consciousness, whereas most mystical
and occult traditions, as well as artistic creation, pay homage to the
moon. Recent discussions of this dichotomy have focused on the operations of the two hemispheres of the brain, the left half embodying
the traditional masculine traits and the right the feminine; though this
line of investigation may eventually give greater psychological precision to the question, it is still useful to speak of solar and lunar consciousness because of its rich symbolic heritage, and all the more so
because the most consistent and obvious pattern of imagery in *The
Recognitions* is the symbolic equation of Rev. Gwyon with the sun and
Camilla with the moon. Making the equation early in the first chapter,
Gaddis proceeds to draw upon the immense religious and mythological
connotations of the sun and moon, effectively enlarging Wyatt's personal struggle for psychic wholeness to universal proportions by em-
ploying archetypal images that have influenced civilization, largely by
way of religion, from the beginning of history. The ubiquity of solar
and lunar imagery in the novel not only converts even atmospheric
conditions into telling indications of Wyatt's psychological state, but
also illuminates and justifies other patterns of imagery and sundry references that otherwise might seem superfluous.

The symbolic alignment of the sun with Rev. Gwyon is introduced
and maintained chiefly by his involvement with Mithraism, a Persian

predecessor and rival of early Christianity, in which the godhead was represented by Sol Invictus, the Invincible Sun. As early as page 8 the reader is informed, with the ironic foreshadowing so common with Gaddis, that at his seminary Gwyon "started the course of mithridatism which was to serve him so well in his later years." We also learn that before he returned to New England after Camilla's funeral he visited the Mithraic temple beneath the basilica at Saint Clement's in Rome (which Gaddis himself finally visited in 1984). Gwyon had squared his shoulders upon "coming forth from the subterranean Mithraeum" (61), convinced Christianity was a forgery of Mithraism, and dedicated himself thereafter not to the Son, but to the Sun. (The pun was not beneath early Christian writers, and Gaddis often plays on the ambiguity.)

But before doing so he, too, receives a supernatural visit from Camilla, where she is symbolically equated with the moon for the first time. At the Real Monasterio de Nuestra Señora de la Otra Vez some two months after his wife's death, he falls ill and develops a delirium:

So he lay alone one evening, perspiring in spite of the cold, almost asleep to be wakened suddenly by the hand of his wife, on his shoulder as she used to wake him. He struggled up from the alcoved bed, across the room to the window where a cold light silently echoed passage. There was the moon, reaching a still arm behind him, to the bed where he had lain. He stood there unsteady in the cold, mumbling syllables which almost resolved into her name, as though he could recall, and summon back, a time before death entered the world, before accident, before magic, and before magic despaired, to become religion. (11–12)

Rev. Gwyon too, then, is offered "passage" to lunar consciousness, but squanders his opportunity. Upon recovering, he resolves to forsake the bleak Christianity of his puritanical community to search for "persistent pattern, and significant form" (15), which he hopes to find in the study of comparative religion. It is enough, he seems to think, to break from the Calvinist tradition of Aunt May and her Use-Me Ladies and to regale his congregation with pagan parallels to their Christianity. But as regards Camilla, he can only hope there will be time (a frequent Prufrockian refrain in the text), and postpones the recovery of what he has lost in her until its recovery is finally beyond reach.

What both he and his son lose in Camilla is the key to the feminine component of the male psyche, what Jung calls the anima. Rev. Gwyon married late in life and only after his own father died (14), suggesting his own upbringing was as stringent as Wyatt's is under Aunt May—a paternal relative, be it noted. That Camilla was antithetical to the repressed life of that patriarchal environment is seen in the two flashbacks in which she appears. In both instances she is portrayed as vital, impulsive, daring, but most of all nourishing: when Camilla noticed her father had mounted the wallpaper upside down, "she threw her arms over his crooked shoulders and thanked him, and never told him" (52). Aunt May or Esther would have pointed out the error immediately. After Camilla's death, however, Rev. Gwyon seems powerless to recoup his losses; he does not consider remarrying—perhaps in obedience to the Mithraic injunction against marrying more than once—and instead buries himself in his studies, apparently feeling things can be set aright if only he can expose Christianity's imposture to his congregation. (Similarly, Wyatt will later assume he can redeem his misdeeds by exposing his forgeries at Brown's party; in both cases, the unenlightened prefer to remain so—a tendency McCandless rails against in *Carpenter's Gothic*.)

The reverend's studies at this time center on the discovery and exposure of antecedents and parallels to Christianity. But he remains impervious to the spiritual nourishment others have found in these same pre-Christian religious traditions. His preoccupation with the "accidents" of religion at the expense of its "substance" (to use, as Gaddis does, the terminology of the Mass) is the same fault, incidentally, that Wittgenstein found with Frazer, on whom Gwyon relies for much of his material. "What narrowness of spiritual life we find in Frazer!" the Austrian philosopher complained. "And as a result: how impossible for him to understand a different way of life from the English one of his time!"[15] An apposite example is Rev. Gwyon's references to the ancient ritual of "drawing down the moon": his interest in the rite is confined to the lurid pagan light it sheds on Matthew 16:19, reducing Jesus to the level of a Thessalonian witch. But this rite, still in use by modern witches, is actually a meditative exercise to enlarge lunar consciousness, to gain access to to the deep wellsprings of the unconscious. It is not the silly superstition Lucian, Aristophanes, and other ancients took it for, but rather, when properly executed, a spiritual exercise akin to Loyola's meditations or the alchemical opus. It may be only an antiquarian curiosity to his father, but Wyatt will eventually recognize the benefits of drawing down the moon.

A declining sun and rising moon are appropriately present at a key event in the first chapter: Wyatt's cure by means of a ritual for the expulsion of evil in an animal scapegoat. Miriam Fuchs has suggested that Rev. Gwyon's sacrifice of his Barbary ape during this ritual masks a sacrifice of Camilla herself, insofar as "this monkey had replaced Camilla" (32), as Aunt May suspected.[16] The obvious parallels to Christ's passion suggest Gwyon sacrifices his wife that his son might live, as the Christian god sacrificed his that Christians might find eternal life.[17] Whether Camilla's spirit transmigrates first into Heracles the ape and later into Esme, as Fuchs argues, or more simply represents Wyatt's anima, it is clear that the sacrificial act is Rev. Gwyon's final break with Camilla. To sacrifice is to give up something dear, and he sacrifices his wife that their son might live. He had turned away from Camilla's photograph at the beginning of the ritual, and afterward never speaks of her death (61). Like Roderick Usher burying his anima in the vault of his unconscious, Rev. Gwyon thereby draws ruin on himself and his house.

What he loses in Camilla he hopes Wyatt may find. Shortly after his recovery, and now lodged in Camilla's sewing room—where "she had come at the moment of death" the narrator reminds us (52)—Wyatt undergoes an experience much like his father's in Spain. That which was offered his father and refused is now offered, indeed forced upon Wyatt. Significantly, Wyatt begins two paintings at this time, each capable of leading him either to salvation or damnation, to Ballima way or Oorooma way (268): a portrait of his mother, and a copy of Bosch's *Seven Deadly Sins.* The first is an attempt to redeem his mother's memory and her rich symbolic heritage, the second a grim emblem of the Calvinist worldview Aunt May tried to impose on him (and eventually the painting that will initiate him into the world of forgery). Both will haunt him throughout the novel.

The painting of Camilla is based on the photograph on the living room mantel (57), and it is important to remember that this photograph was made before Camilla was married (19). Much is made of Camilla's symbolic virginity in the first chapter: she is said to have "borne Gwyon a son and gone, virginal, to earth: virginal in the sight of man, at any rate" (14)—because Gwyon arranges to have her transported in a white funeral carriage "ordained for infants and maidens." For Wyatt, Camilla remains "his virgin mother" (19) and thus is not the impulsive New England girl who married his father, but rather the idealized figure Graves calls the White Goddess—at once girl, mother, and hag, and patroness of the white magic of art.

At the end of the first chapter, then, Wyatt must choose between the Christian myth of the Father and Son (embodied in Rev. Gwyon, "for somehow his father and the Lord were the same person" [20]) and the ancient cult of the White Goddess and her son, the artist–priest. Instead of finishing the portrait of his mother, however, he first finishes the Bosch forgery, which he sells to Recktall Brown to finance his trip to Europe to study art. Thereafter, the incomplete portrait of Camilla (until its destruction by fire sends him to Spain for the "original"), along with her Byzantine earrings that his father passes on to him, will be a reminder of his incomplete relationship with his mother/anima, which will in turn prevent him from having a complete relationship with any other woman ("Finish it," Esther will plead. "Then there might be room for me" [88]). There is no ruse Wyatt will disdain henceforth to avoid coming to terms with his mother and all she represents. Camilla will remain "in cold vigilance, waiting" like the moon (61) while her son squanders his inheritance and attempts to forge an existence in which she need not play a part, until he realizes only she can supply the missing part of him without which he has no real existence.

The World of Night

Writing from Munich, Wyatt tells his father he cannot continue studying for the ministry because of guilt, and like a guilty criminal Wyatt goes underground. Much is made throughout the novel of the fact that Wyatt paints at night, evoking the traditional associations of night: death, sin, guilt, fear, crime, sex, and—not so traditional— artistic creation. In "the darkening room" of Wyatt's Paris studio, the art critic Crémer reminds Wyatt of Degas's remark "that the artist must approach his work in the same frame of mind in which the criminal commits his deed" (71). When Esther surprises Wyatt in his New York studio years later, he stands "as though stricken, in the midst of some criminal commission" (87) and she wonders if "the music of Handel [would] always recall sinful commission, the perpetration of some crime in illumined darkness, recognized as criminal only by him who committed it" (98). Esther maligns "this crazy Calvinistic secrecy, sin" (129), but when Valentine makes the same charge, Wyatt defends himself: "It isn't so simple. [. . .] It's the same sense . . . yes, this sense of a blue day in summer, do you understand? It's too much, such a day, it's too fully illuminated. It's defeating that way, it doesn't allow you to project this illumination yourself, this . . . selective illumination that's necessary to paint" (239–40).

The recurrence of the word "illumination" in some of these quotations is significant, for the word implies intellectual enlightenment
along with its root meaning, and reminds us that the paradox out of
darkness comes illumination is a major premise of mysticism, alchemy,
and (Wyatt insists) artistic creation. However, Wyatt's defense has an
air of rationalization about it, for he is prey to the very guilt and
secrecy of which he is accused. Aunt May made it quite clear to him
that artists are of the devil's party, and Wyatt never does completely
free himself from her influence; two pages before his final disappearance he is still quoting her on "the prospect of sin" (898, from 33).
Young Wyatt's earliest artistic efforts had to be carried out in secrecy—
not only his drawings hidden in the midden heap but his first forgery
as well—and the counterfeit nature of the older Wyatt's work of course
necessitates both secrecy and guilt, despite his rationalizations. Aunt
May was Wyatt's first and most severe critic, and he has apparently
never forgotten her reaction to his first drawing: "—Don't you love our
Lord Jesus, after all? He said he did. —Then why do you try to take
His place? Our Lord is the only true creator, and only sinful people try
to emulate Him. [. . .] That is why Satan is the Fallen Angel, for
he rebelled when he tried to emulate Our Lord Jesus. And he won his
own domain, didn't he. Didn't he! And his own light is the light of
the fires of Hell! Is that what you want?" (34).[18] Here, illumination
comes by the light of the fires of hell and reinforces in young Wyatt's
mind the relationship between artistic creation and sin.

Yet night is also the domain of the female, ruled by Goethe's Mother
Night, and associated in myth and psychology with the unconscious—
an association the narrator spells out quite often (e.g., 12, 53, 69,
891, 955). Drawn to the night, Wyatt is also terrified of it, terrified
of confronting the dark contents of his unconscious. The victim of
nightmares, he often works at night to avoid dreaming, which entails
entering "the world of night, [where] lost souls clutching guidebooks
follow the sun through subterranean passage gloom, corridors dark and
dangerous: so the king built his tomb deep in earth, and alone wanders
the darkness of death there through twenty-four thousand square feet
of passages and halls, stairs, chambers and pits. So Egypt" (388), and
so the unconscious.

Confrontation with the dangerous unconscious usually takes the psy-
chomythological forms of an infernal descent or a vigil through the
dark night of the soul. The number of works mentioned or alluded to
in *The Recognitions* that feature one or the other of these related themes
is extensive: Goethe's *Faust* (opening with the Doctor's dark night of

the soul and later involving an infernal descent to the Mothers),
Dante's *Inferno,* the *Dark Night of the Soul* of Saint John of the Cross,
the apocryphal *Acts of Pilate* (the second part of which features the
harrowing of hell), Homer's *Odyssey* (book 11), Vergil's *Aeneid* (book
6), Fichte's *Vocation of Man* (book 2), the Egyptian *Book of the Dead,*
Rimbaud's *A Season in Hell,* Gluck's *Orfeo ed Euridice,* Ibsen's *Peer Gynt,*
Novalis's *Hymn to the Night,* the medieval passion play *The Harrow of
Hell,* Marlowe's *Doctor Faustus,* and many others. In addition, numerous references are made to myths dealing with the underworld, which
brings in another important association—the equation of night with
hell. As long as Wyatt's psychological conflicts remain unresolved, he
remains in hell, so to speak. Wyatt had been dwelling in an "infernal
kingdom" (98) ever since his arrival in New York City, and numerous
indirect, even casual references reinforce this symbolic equation, building upon the poetic tradition linking the modern city with hell (Milton, Blake, Francis Thompson, Eliot, and later Allen Ginsberg). The
city is called "Dis" (696), a "chilly hell" (467), and the discovery of
Wyatt's two Bouts forgeries takes place, appropriately enough, in
Hell's Kitchen (288). Wyatt moves from uptown to downtown when
he begins his forgeries, and is rumored to be living "underground"
(172). Even expletives contribute: "You look like hell," Brown tells
Wyatt at one point, who responds, "That's because I'm . . . I've been
working like hell" (238). Like Milton's Satan, he seems on the verge
of lamenting, "Which way I fly is Hell; myself am Hell" (*Paradise Lost,*
4.75). Consequently, when he decides to return to New York from
New England and expose his forgeries, he refers to it as "the harrowing
of hell" (442).

Escaping from New York, Wyatt leaves both the underworld and
the world of night for Spain, a purgatory where night gives way to a
succession of overcast, "sunless" days as Wyatt works through his guilt.
"The even unchanging gray of the sky" (806) in these Spanish chapters
represents a provisional union of bright day and dark night, a conjunction of the two extremes between which Wyatt had been fluctuating throughout the novel. Only on the final day does dawn bring a
clear sky; throughout the novel Wyatt had been waking at dusk and
mistaking it for dawn, but finally he wakes at dawn, mistaking it for
dusk at first, but learning quickly "the sky wasn't getting darker, it
was getting light" (893–94). His long dark night of the soul over, the
Pleiades signaling the beginning of a new sailing season (892), Wyatt/
Stephen is ready for a new voyage: "Now at last, to live deliberately"
(900).

This Pelagian Atmosphere

In mythology, the movement of the moon across the sky was most often compared to a ship at sea, and illustrations of moon boats have survived from many early cultures. The sky has impressed many as an immense celestial sea, and even in our technological day space exploration employs traditional nautical terminology. A third large pattern of mythic imagery in *The Recognitions* is generated from the metaphoric identification of the sea with the sky, which in light of the relationship between the lunar and nocturnal symbolism examined so far, can perhaps be best understood as yet another facet of what slowly emerges as a huge, interrelated system of cosmological symbolism, again extending to universal proportions the inner struggles of an individual.

The night sea journey common to so many myths represents yet another confrontation with the unconscious, and more specifically with the anima (since the sea is a universally recognized feminine symbol). Gaddis builds on this archetypal symbolism, augmenting it with a wide and colorful array of background material, to establish one of the major themes of the novel, that of voyaging. A voyage implies a homecoming—"whoever started a journey, without the return in the front of his mind?" (898)—and Wyatt's ultimate destination is the resolution of the interior conflicts preventing him from leading a fulfilling life. Gaddis wrote in his notes for *The Recognitions,* "I think this book will have to be on voyaging, all the myth & metaphor of that in modern times."[19] A heavy cargo of "myth & metaphor" accompanies Wyatt on his voyage, largely through Gaddis's multiplying of the metaphoric possibilities of the sea until it floods the novel with a "pelagian atmosphere" (553).

The novel begins literally at sea, and the allure of voyaging and the conceit of a celestial sea are introduced as early as page 6 in a discussion of the constellation Argo and the Pleiades. (It is worth noting that the novel opens with the setting of the Pleiades and ends with their rising, symbolic of the general movement of the novel from death to rebirth, from the Day of the Dead to Easter Sunday.) Throughout the first chapter, there are many references to voyaging—especially from the Town Carpenter, Wyatt's maternal grandfather—but also several deliberate blurrings of sky, sea, and land: the harsh plain of Castile is compared to the sea (7; cf. 770); the sky at the time of Wyatt's departure for divinity school is described as "deep gray-blue, banded with the colors of rust seen under water" (60); in their awkwardness during this scene, both Rev. Gwyon and Wyatt are "caught, as a swimmer on the surface is caught by that cold current whose suddenness snares him in cramps and sends him in dumb surprise to the bottom" (60); and there is the first of many references to Gervase of Tilbury's tale of "the sky being a sea, the celestial sea, and a man coming down a rope to undo an anchor that's gotten caught on a tombstone" (28). Even the Town Carpenter's interest in ballooning advances the conceit of a voyage in a celestial sea.

But this traditional conceit soon takes on a number of unexpected overtones. Young Wyatt associates the drowned sailor of Gervase's tale with the martyrdom of Saint Clement by way of the anchor common to both stories (44), to which the older Wyatt adds a third element, namely Charles Fort's wry speculation that perhaps we are all at the bottom of a celestial sea and are occasionally fished for by aliens, a speculation that Wyatt (and Esme after him) will voice often in the novel. These three references join in the general submarine imagery that accumulates (see 60, 79, 109, 115) until it is rumored that Wyatt "lives underground. Or underwater" (172). A number of similar references follow until, arguing with Valentine the night he decides to return home to his father, Wyatt brings these references into a Christian perspective:

—Now, remember? Who was it, "gettato a mare," remember? an anchor tied to his neck? and thrown, caught by kelpies and martyred, remember? in the celestial sea. Here, maybe we're fished for. [. . .] Have you read Averroes? What I mean is, do we believe in order to understand? Or in order to be . . . fished for. [. . .] Yes, yes, that's it. That's it! Flesh, remember? flesh, how thou art fishified. He jumped to his feet. —Listen, do you understand? We're fished for! On this rock, remember? and I shall make thee a fisher of men? (382)

Suddenly recalling Jesus' promise to Peter and Andrew to make them fishers of men—salvaged from this mélange of medieval tales, scholastic argument, even a line from *Romeo and Juliet* (2.4.37)—Wyatt decides to return home to resume his studies for the ministry. A number of nautical references in the chapter at home, however, indicate that Wyatt is not yet out of the sea, that is, no closer to salvation than he was before. Undersea imagery continues throughout part 2, especially at Brown's, fancifully identified as the undersea domain of Ibsen's Troll King.

In part 3, Esme associates Wyatt both with the drowned sailor retrieved from the ocean during her and Stanley's voyage (834) and with the drowned sailor of Gervase's tale (912, 914). The first association is of vital importance, for it represents Wyatt's symbolic death at sea, foreshadowed several times earlier in the novel. Wyatt's "drowning" takes place in the chapter strategically placed between his abandonment of Sinisterra and their "mummy" as Stephan Asche in III.3 and his reemergence in III.5 as simply Stephen, the name originally intended for him by Camilla. An obvious parallel is the "Death by Water" section that appears at about the same point structurally in Eliot's *The Waste Land,* the symbolic death prerequisite to rebirth. "I've been a voyage, I'll tell you," Wyatt/Stephen concludes at the end. "I've been a voyage starting at the bottom of the sea" (895).

In contrast to the lunar and nocturnal symbolism, both deployed in a fairly straightforward fashion, the marine imagery is developed through the novel in a variety of ingenious ways. An informative example is Gaddis's extended pun on Pelagianism / pelagic / pelagian / Pelagia. Pelagianism, it will be remembered, is one of the heresies Wyatt asks his father about after his return from a year's theological studies. One of the great heresiarchs, the British monk Pelagius (ca. 360–420) not only denied the doctrine of original sin but insisted that man is free to do good or evil—as opposed to the Augustinian doctrine that man, without spiritual guidance, is irresistibly drawn to evil. Rev. Gwyon minimizes Pelagius's achievement: "If it hadn't been Pelagius it would have been someone else. But by now we . . . too many of us may embrace original sin ourselves to explain our own guilt, and behave . . . treat everyone else as though they were full-fledged . . . umm . . . Pelagians doing just as they please" (58). Wyatt himself, as he confesses later, is a Pelagian (806), though that hardly means he simply does as he pleases. Rather, it means he takes personal responsibility for his own salvation, refusing to rely on Christ (or his ministers) to do it for him. Too confident a reliance on Christ, Pelagius argued, promotes "moral decline."[20]

The name "Pelagius" is a Latinized form of the heretic's Welsh name Morgan, meaning "the sea"; Gaddis may or may not be playing on the connection between Pelagius and the sea when Wyatt puns on "Pelagic miles distant" (392), but he surely is during Basil Valentine's harangue:

—And what was it you said? A man's damnation is his own damned business? It's not true, you know. It's not true. Why, good heavens, this suicide of yours? [. . .] Look! Look there, in the sky where it's still blue, that line? That white line the airplane's drawn, do you see it? how the wind's billowed it out like rope in a current of water? Yes, your man in the celestial sea, eh? coming down to undo it, down to the bottom, and they find him dead as though drowned. Why, this . . . pelagian atmosphere of yours, you know. Homicide, was it? (553)

"A man's damnation is his own damned business" might be construed as a clever if grim epigram summarizing the Pelagian heresy, but Valentine's use of "pelagian" in reference to Wyatt's celestial sea obsession suggests that Valentine plays Saint Augustine to Wyatt's Pelagius in the novel's theological debate. Wyatt undertakes his own salvation by taking the part of sacrifical priest: Valentine had accused him a few pages earlier of wanting to commit suicide by exposing his forgeries, but Wyatt had answered, "Suicide? this? Do you think there's only one self, then? that this isn't homicide? closer to homicide?" (546). As Valentine recognizes a few lines later, the self Wyatt wants to kill is "the old man," a New Testament locution (Eph. 4:22, Col. 3:9) that refers to the sinful self before baptism. (Otto and Sinisterra use this phrase as well.) Wyatt is both priest and sacrifical victim, pushing Pelagianism to a theological extreme that also includes his father and Our Father among the old men he needs to kill to attain salvation.

Pelagia is also the name of one of the courtesan saints Wyatt recalls during his interior monologue at the point when revulsion from the sins of the flesh is uppermost in mind (392, eight lines before "Pelagic miles distant"). This *"bienheureuse pécheresse"* (blessed sinner), as Gaddis's source calls her,[21] began her career as a different sort of fisher of men, a suitable figure in the woman-as-temptress theme of Wyatt's meditations—a theme that finds expression in the novel's mermaid motif, the most exotic element of its marine imagery. Ungallantly introduced with references to various "faked" mermaids (16, 65—anything can be faked in this novel), the mermaid next surfaces in a conversation between Wyatt and Fuller, Brown's West Indian servant and one of Gaddis's great comic inventions. Contrasting his easy belief in mermaids to the difficulty of faith, Fuller ingenuously concludes:

—It remain a challenge to believe, always. Not so simple to accept, like the mermaids.
    —The mermaids . . . the mermaids . . .
    —Yes, sar.

—And you can . . . accept the mermaids, without much difficulty?

—Yes, sar, though they remain the complication of the mermaid mahns.

—Yes, there does.

—But the mermaid womans . . .

—Yes, the women . . . you can believe in the women . . .

—Oh yes sar, Fuller said, and then after a pause, —Woman bring you into the world, you got to stick with her.

—Wasn't it woman brought evil into the world, then?

—Sar?

—Yes. When she picked the fruit from the forbidden tree; and gave it to the man to eat?

—So the evil already there provided, and quite naturally she discover it.

—Yes, yes, and she gave it to the man . . .

—She share it with him, sar, said Fuller. —Thaht the reason why we love her. (348–49)

The image of mermaids remains with Wyatt; after his fruitless discussion with Brown—in which he seems to identify his own difficulties with "the complication of the mermaid men" (361)—Wyatt tells Valentine he has been "consorting with mermaids in the bottom of a tank where the troll king lives" (375), conflating one legend with another (as we have seen him do before), this time Peer Gynt's visit to the mountain fortress of the Troll King with the Frog King who lives at the bottom of a well in the Grimm Brothers' tale Esme had read aloud to Wyatt earlier (273). I have already quoted Wyatt's reference to kelpies (382), the Scottish branch of the mermaid family. In one sense, all of the women Wyatt consorts with are mermaids, sisters to the sirens of classical mythology, representing the beautiful but dangerous aspect of the feminine, luring the male down into the watery unconscious and sensuality, away from solar consciousness and intellection.[22]

It is this misogynistic fear that causes Wyatt to flee the intimacy Esme offers to return to the patriarchal world of his fathers, only to discover that his father has gone mad. From two others on the border of madness, however, Wyatt receives valuable advice. "Something amiss," the Town Carpenter tells him, "we must simplify" (441);[23] and when Wyatt questions the stigmaticist serving girl, Janet, on the meaning of damnation, she defines it simply, "That is life without love" (442). With these words in mind, Wyatt boards the next train back to New York to expose his forgeries and to accept the love Esme had offered, hoping in both actions to escape damnation and find salvation.

Wyatt's evil angel, however, mocks him for thinking salvation can be found in a woman:

Basil Valentine turned and laughed in his face. —Really, really my dear fellow. No, he said, clutching the single gray glove before him. —The "somber glow" at the end of the second act, is it? the duet with Senta, is that it? . . . "the somber glow, no, it is salvation that I crave," eh! "Might such an angel come, my soul to save," your Flying Dutchman sings, eh? Good heavens! And up they go to heaven in a wave, or whatever it was? Really! And all that foolishness you were carrying on with the last time I saw you, that "I min Tro . . . " and the rest of it, that Where has he been all this time? and your Solveig answers In my faith? In my hope? In my, . . . good heavens! You are romantic, aren't you! If you do think you mean all this? And then what, They lived happily forever after? (551)

This important concept of woman as the means for salvation was introduced as early as the second chapter in the first description of Wyatt's wife, Esther: "Still, like other women in love, salvation was her original purpose, redemption her eventual privilege; and, like most women, she could not wait to see him thoroughly damned first, before she stepped in, believing, perhaps as they do, that if he were saved now he would never need to be redeemed" (78). The concept is maintained with the identification of both Camilla and Esme with the Virgin Mary, the archetype of salvation via the female; and as late as III.3, Wyatt is tempted to hang his hopes of salvation on Pastora and their possible daughter.

Although endorsing Pelagius's admonition against relying too heavily on Christ for personal salvation, Wyatt has slipped into the more romantic notion of relying on women for the same purpose—the danger of which is set out by Denis de Rougemont in his *Love in the Western World,* another of Gaddis's sources. But by the end of the novel Wyatt/Stephen seems to have realized that the female promise of redemption is as illusory as a mermaid's promise of love to homesick sailors: both lead to destruction and the loss of self—or at the very least to a loss of independence and self-reliance, advocated in the copy of Thoreau that Wyatt carries around. Both the Flying Dutchman and Peer Gynt perish as they find salvation in a woman's embrace. "Yes, the women," Wyatt had said earlier in that discussion with Fuller, "you can believe in the women" and apparently agrees that "Women bring you into the world, you got to stick with her" (348). But this cannot be at the expense of one's individuality, one's autonomy, which the female—in her destructive/unconscious aspect symbolized here by the mermaid—often threatens. The sparse but psychologically precise use of mermaid imagery, then, strengthens the identification of the sea with the unconscious and further defines the role of the female in Wyatt's "voyage starting at the bottom of the sea."

As mentioned earlier, a "pelagian atmosphere" is maintained throughout the novel not only with marine imagery but with dozens of similes comparing the land to sea and actions on land to actions on/in/under the ocean. And not only is the sea often compared to the sky, as we have seen, but there are several deliberate confusions of sky and land (e.g., 205–6, 790, 899), so that a symbolic equation of ocean = land = sky = ocean is made. By deliberately confusing both the land and sky with the sea, Gaddis is able to give almost all of Wyatt's actions the trappings of a sea voyage. Appropriately enough, none of Wyatt's actual ocean voyages is dramatized; only those of the other characters are. Thus the symbolic nature of his voyage is emphasized over the merely literal. For even though he does indeed voyage in a literal sense, the novel is the story of his psychological voyage— like those of Peer Gynt, Odysseus, the Flying Dutchman, and the Wandering Jew across the world, Faust to the Mothers, and Dante, Christ, and Orpheus to hell—a voyage through the unconscious but dominant elements of his psyche.

Thus a vast, interlocking network of maternal symbolism pervades the novel, all generated from the psychic havoc that resulted from Wyatt's early separation from his mother (and paralleled historically in the conquest of matriarchal religion and sensibility by the patriarchal) and his subsequent guilt over dishonoring her with his forgeries. Sea, earth, moon, night, sky, hell—all are feminine symbols conspiring against him. Robert Graves, whose *White Goddess* greatly influenced Gaddis, argues that the male must exist in an essentially female universe, and thus should pay homage to the Eternal Feminine, not rebel with sterile masculine rationality. (And by "rationality" both Graves and Gaddis mean "thinking along prescribed lines without any thought for sensibility."[24]) Wyatt is immersed in a world of female symbols, yet spends most of his life denying that world.

"We must never forget," Jung reminds us, "in the case of the anima, that it is a question of psychic facts which have never before been in man's psychological possession; that hitherto were always to be found outside his consciousness in every possible form of projection."[25] Gaddis's matrix of feminine symbols represents every possible form of projection of those qualities Wyatt keeps at arm's length for so long: emotion, intuition, tenderness, even irrationality. Early in the novel, Esther often complains of Wyatt's lack of emotion and his overreliance on things of the intellect. "I wish you *would* lose your temper," she tells him at one point, "or *some*thing because this . . . this restraint, this pose, this control that you've cultivated, Wyatt, it becomes inhuman" (97). Complaining of Wyatt's coldly rational reaction to Bach's ebullient Suite No. 1 in C, she tells Otto, "Yes but it isn't human [. . .]. It isn't a way to live." Otto comforts her with "He can't just go on, like this" (126), nor does he. Wyatt himself realizes something is wrong, something is missing, symbolized by the missing mother. The unconscious presence of Camilla throughout the novel represents the lure of the irrational, of the need to balance the intellect with emotion, reason with intuition. In fact, it is significant that the only dramatic portrayal of Camilla in the book is in a flashback to the time when Rev. Gwyon's archaeologist friend offered her a pair of Byzantine earrings, "not knowing Camilla, not knowing she would run from the room clutching the gold hoops, and surprised (though Gwyon was not) when she burst in again with wild luster in her eyes, wearing the gold earrings, blood all over them" (14). Marrying Camilla had been Gwyon's attempt at tempering the intellect with emotion; he passes on this legacy to his son by giving him her earrings as keepsakes, which Wyatt simply keeps in a box, just as he keeps his emotions in a box. (The earrings represent the mother as the razor does the father; but as golden circles, they represent authenticity and wholeness, while the razor represents castration and conformity to Christian principles—see the Saint Wulstan anecdote [203].)

Esme discovers the earrings and dons them, but Wyatt has already spurned her by that point. Not until the last page on which he appears does he realize the importance of the earrings; by intending to pass them on to his daughter,[26] he demonstrates his recognition of the emotions and especially of the strongest, most liberating emotion of all, love. Not the sentimental love of romantics, nor the lust of sensualists: the kind of love Wyatt embraces is less eros than agape—charity, attentiveness, caring. "Charity's the challenge" Wyatt had admitted earlier (383), but not until the end of the novel is he psychologically prepared to commit himself to this challenge. It is important to note that the Augustinian motto Wyatt chooses reads "Dilige et quod vis

fac" ("Love, and do what you want to" [899]), not the more popular
form "Amo et fac quod vis"—that is, Wyatt prefers the verb meaning
"to esteem and care for" over that meaning "to love passionately."[27]
This is the kind of love recommended in Eliot's *Four Quartets*; for Wyatt
it represents a new beginning, not an end, for as Eliot argues, this
form of love never ceases to be a challenge.

Chapter Three
The Recognitions:
The Self Who Can Do More

Although Wyatt's quest is the center of attention in *The Recognitions,* he appears only in half of the novel's twenty-two chapters, and even in some of these makes only fleeting appearances. As Gaddis stated in one of his notes, "the body of the novel has not been squarely about [Wyatt], it has been about the others, and he only insofar as he was the spirit they lost."[1] Just as Camilla, the spirit Wyatt lost, keeps "cold vigilance, waiting" (61) for Wyatt to rectify his imperfections, he does so for others: "I wait," he tells Valentine, describing his role in their hypothetical novel (a metafictional version of *The Recognitions*). "Where is he? Listen, he's there all the time. None of them moves, but it reflects him, none of them . . . reacts, but to react with him, none of them hates but to hate with him, to hate him, and loving . . . none of them loves, but, loving . . . " (263). Here Wyatt founders, aware of the absence of love in his life, but for the others he epitomizes what Valentine calls "this other . . . more beautiful self who . . . can do more than they can" (253).

Each of the novel's major characters sees in Wyatt what he or she might have become: "the self-who-can-do-more," to quote again from Gaddis's notes, "the creative self if it had not been killed by the other, in Valentine's case, Reason; in Brown's case, material gain; in Otto's case, vanity and ambition; in Stanley's case, the Church; in Anselm's case, religion, &c. &c."[2] Like Rilke's angel, with whom Wyatt is several times associated, he represents for these characters "a being in whom the limitations and contradictions of present human nature have been transcended, a being in whom thought and action, insight and achievement, will and capability, the actual and the ideal, are one."[3] As we have seen, Wyatt is no angel and has difficulties of his own reaching the Rilkean ideal, but he does possess enough talent to remind others of their shortcomings. Otto, for example, is lost in envy and admiration: "I mean to know as much as you do, it must be . . .

I mean you can really do anything you want to by now, I mean, you don't feel all sort of hedged in by the parts you don't know about, like I do" (134). "It was like a part of me working, like a part of myself working there," Wyatt's former supervisor Benny reminisces. "And I couldn't do it. He could do it and I couldn't do it" (606). This sense of failure and inadequacy dogs most of the novel's other characters as well, driving them to madness, drugs and alcohol, inertia, suicide, or at the best to what Thoreau calls lives of quiet desperation.

These characters also provide a certain amount of dramatic comic relief from Wyatt's grimly serious quest for redemption and authenticity. With the same kind of "calamitous wit" he ascribes to Saul Bellow,[4] Gaddis may have intended a comedy of manners that deflates the lives and pretensions of the New York intellectuals, literati, artsy homosexuals, and assorted camp followers who make up his dramatis personae. But the ferocity of Gaddis's satire, the contempt he heaps upon nearly everyone in the novel, betrays the stern moralist who doesn't so much invite the reader to laugh at the human foibles of his characters as to recoil in horror and inquire of them, aghast with indignation, "But why do you do the things you do? Why do you live the life you live?" (923). This half of *The Recognitions* is less a comedy than a tragedy of manners.

Gaddis accomplishes much more than an exposé of Bohemian life; instead, he offers a dramatization of the sociological pressures that drive people to don masks, to exchange "the things worth being for the things worth having" (499), to confuse the genuine with the counterfeit, and to reject "revelation for fear of examining the motives which conspired to breed it" (613). Gaddis's own relentless inquiry into those motives makes well-rounded characters of what may first appear to be caricatures, mere butts of his satirical thrusts. "How little of us ever meets how little of another" Agnes Deigh complains in her suicide letter to Dr. Weisgall (758), and how little attention has been paid to this intriguing gallery of characters.

Otto

In Gaddis's "bop version" of *Faust,* Otto Pivner plays Wagner to Wyatt's magus in the early part of the novel, but thereafter acts more as a comic double, a funhouse mirror reflection of the "refugee artist" (661). Like the clown in a Shakespearean subplot, Otto functions as a ludicrous counterpart to Wyatt, aping his manner, stealing his best lines, parodying Wyatt's quest as his does older models. Dozens of parallel situations link the two: Otto cuts his cheek (449) and asks his presumed father (515) the same question that Wyatt, also with torn cheek, asks his father (427); a bartender calls after Otto to remind him of his abandoned newspaper (475) just as a French waiter had called after Wyatt about his (77); Otto's hair starts burning (486) as Wyatt often dreams his does (87, 99, 586); Otto's final conversation with Esther (609–13, 620–22) echoes Wyatt's last conversation with her (585–92) so closely that Esther can prompt him; during those conversations both Wyatt (589) and Otto (620) remark that, looking around, there doesn't seem much worth doing anymore; Otto's last conscious act is to pound on a church door seeking sanctuary (729), just as Wyatt does before being turned away from his monastery (891); by the end of the novel each is called by a new name—Otto as Gordon, Wyatt as Stephen—and the final appearance of each is accompanied by the ringing of church bells (900, 950). These are only a few of the countless parallels, echoes, and parodies Gaddis scatters throughout the text, giving Otto's actions the same kind of vague familiarity that nags the readers of his plagiarized play—whose title, appropriately enough, he stole from Wyatt.

Otto's stumbling progess is not played entirely for laughs, however. His troubles with identity and authenticity not only are mundane variations on Wyatt's more metaphysical ones, but are closer to the plane most readers inhabit than the rarified one on which Wyatt operates. Similarly, his vanity may only be a more common version of the intense self-consciousness and introspection that characterizes Wyatt's thoughts, who can even be said to be guilty of theological vanity when he demands of his father, *"Am I the man for whom Christ died?"* (440). In his fumbling way, Otto even approaches the same "recognitions" Wyatt makes, often by way of the same metaphors from painting. In one of the most significant passages in the novel, Otto tells Esme

—a story I heard once, a friend of mine told me, somebody I used to know, a story about a forged painting. It was a forged Titian that somebody had painted over another old painting, when they scraped the forged Titian away they found some worthless old painting underneath it, the forger had used it because it was an old canvas. But then there was something under that worthless painting, and they scraped it off and underneath that they found a Titian, a real Titian that had been there all the time. It was as though when the forger was working, and he didn't know the original was underneath, I mean he didn't know he knew it, but it knew, I mean something knew. I mean, do you see what I mean? That underneath that the original is there, that the real . . . thing is there, and on the surface you . . . if you can only . . . see what I mean? (450–51)

In a later conversation with Esther Otto employs the same metaphors from counterfeiting that have bedeviled Wyatt, using them in conjunction with the talismanic verb "to recognize": "And this, this mess, ransacking this mess looking for your own feelings and trying to rescue them but it's too late, you can't even recognize them when they come to the surface because they've been spent everywhere and, vulgarized and exploited and wasted and spent wherever we could, they keep demanding and you keep paying and you can't . . . and then all of a sudden somebody asks you to pay in gold and you can't. Yes, you can't, you haven't got it, and you can't" (621–22).

These are two of several instances where Otto's insights come close to matching Wyatt's, but each time Otto backs off "with the brave refusal of one rejecting revelation for fear of examining the motives which conspired to breed it" (613). The kind of wholesale revision of one's life that Wyatt/Stephen makes is too drastic a move for most of us, and yet even Otto may be ready to make such a change by the end of the novel: learning that Jesse has run off with his counterfeit money, Otto/Gordon reacts to the doctor's injunction "You'll have to start all over again" by tearing off his bandages and laughing, with "a soft wind from the south, and the bells ringing a morning Angelus" (950) to suggest he too is ready to begin a new life.

Before reaching this point, however, Otto traverses his own inferno. He is first seen in a Lexington Avenue bar gazing blankly at what will emerge as a symbolic triad: "staring at a dollar bill pinned on the wall, a sign which said, *If you drive your* FATHER *to drink drive him here,* and his own image in the mirror" (101). Worrying about money, his father, and his image are Otto's major concerns in the novel, and the ridiculous circumstances in which this symbolic triad is introduced sets the tone for most of his actions. Having recently arrived in New York City from Harvard, poor in money but rich in vanity and ambition, Otto enters the world of Wyatt and his wife with the first of many fabrications: overhearing a barfly yell at a man in a Santa Claus suit, "Hey Pollyotch, don't start singing your ladonnamobilay in here" (101), Otto revises this for Esther when telling her "he'd been at a party uptown, at some playwright's house, he left when it got too noisy and

some woman kept calling him Pagliacci" (105). Although Esther
quickly sees through him as "a conceited pretentious boy" (106), she
finds his attentions to her consoling as Wyatt withdraws further into
himself.

She grows annoyed soon enough, however, with his obsession with
money and makes the acute observation, "You seem to take not having
it as a reflection on your manhood," to which Otto responds, "But
money, I mean, damn it, a man does feel castrated in New York without money" (150–51). Later, Max taunts him, "You have a real complex about money don't you Otto, a real castration complex without
it" (463), which Gaddis brings to a comic apotheosis when Otto goes
to meet his father for the first time since childhood. Panicking at the
loss of his wallet while trying to pick up a blonde in a bar, Otto "felt
for his inside breast pocket, as though the wallet must have been there
all the time, its absence illusory, caused by witchcraft; and he glanced
quickly at the blonde, as those medieval inquisitors, fingering the
pages of the *Malleus Maleficarum* may have glanced at the witches who
seemed to deprive men of their virile members, when they found that
'such members are never actually taken away from the body, but are
only hidden by a glamour from the senses of sight and touch'" (512).
When his "father" gives him his "Christmas present"—actually forger
Frank Sinisterra passing $5,000 in counterfeit twenties to his pre-
sumed contact—Otto keeps "the packet clutched against his parts"
(520) then rushes up to his hotel room to spread the money over his
bed with the ardor of an impassioned lover, "counting the money, in
various positions" (521). This money, of course, proves his downfall:
learning of its counterfeit nature, he flees the country with it, gets
wounded in earnest in a Central American revolution (after faking such
a wound through most of the book), and finds the freedom of cathartic
laughter only when he discovers the tainted money has been stolen
from him.

Otto's search for a father is as hapless as his search for wealth, and
in fact financial rather than filial motives lead him to arrange to meet
the father he hasn't seen since childhood. No explanation is given for
the long estrangement, and Otto shows some trepidation at the prospect of meeting Mr. Pivner. "It was a problem until now more easily
left unsolved; and be damned to Oedipus and all the rest of them. For
now, the father might be anyone the son chose" (303). Needless to say,
he chooses badly. Sitting in a hotel lobby awaiting his father, trying
to guess if Mr. Pivner is among those present, Otto chooses a gentle-

man he later catches in bed with the blonde Otto had hoped to pick up, a woman who will later sag encouragingly in Mr. Pivner's direction—all adding to the Oedipal tension surrounding Wyatt's relation to his father. With a Dickensian relish for coincidence and mistaken identity, Gaddis propels Frank Sinisterra into the lobby just as Mr. Pivner is being led away as a suspected junkie and both Otto and Sinisterra make the logical mistake, with hilarious results. (In Gaddis's small world, Sinisterra not only is responsible for the death of Camilla but is the real father of Chaby Sinisterra, Otto's seedy rival for Esme, who, unbeknownst to either of them, is hopelessly in love with Wyatt. A temporary father to Otto, Sinisterra will also become one to Wyatt later in the novel.) Sincere in his desire to be reunited with his son, Mr. Pivner returns to the hotel the following night, and finds himself in the lavatory standing next to a "figure his own height, near the same stature, [. . .] when the whole face turned on him, turned bloodshot eyes in a desolation of contempt" (566–67). Mr. Pivner's hopes flicker but quickly go out as no recognition takes place, and he soon finds a surrogate son in the affably fatuous Eddie Zefnic.

Like "Oedipus and all the rest of them," Otto is engaged in an archetypal quest, but as John Seelye points out, "the plotting of this incident recalls Restoration comedy"[5] more than it does the spiritual quests of Oedipus, Hamlet, Ishmael, Stephen Dedalus, or, more to the point, Wyatt Gwyon. Otto's motives for finding his father have nothing to do with love, atonement, or spiritual kinship, and in fact extend little beyond the anticipation of a generous Christmas present (preferaby in cash) and listening to his patrician (if not regal) father speak of "his intimacies with opera stars, artists, producers, over breast of guinea hen and wine" (518). Similarly, Otto's numerous encounters with mirrors are not numinous opportunities for the "intimacies of catoptric communion" (673) as they are for Wyatt and Esme, but vain attempts to prepare a face to meet the faces he hopes to meet: "He smiled at himself in the mirror. He raised an eyebrow. Better. He moistened his lips, and curled the upper one. Better still. The smile, which had shown his face obsequious, was gone. He must remember this arrangement: left eyebrow raised, eyelids slightly drawn, lips moistened, parted, down at corners. This was the expression for New York" (159–60).

As Otto progresses through the novel, wrapping himself tighter and tighter in the web of deceptions, betrayals, and self-fabrications he has spun around himself, his mirror image records the assaults on his increasingly fragmented identity. Noting that Esme has finally put up a mirror in her apartment, he glances "into it to see his face shorn off at the jaw" (480). A few hours earlier, Otto had been seated in a bar staring "straight before him; but he did not see his face for the sign FRANKS AND KRAUT 20¢ was pasted on the mirror just above his collar" (474). The next time Otto stares into a bar mirror, it takes "him a good half-minute to realize that neither the stubbled chin, nor the flattened nose, nor the bunched ears, nor the yellow eyes he stared into, were his own" (486). While Wyatt struggles toward psychic integration, Otto disintegrates so rapidly that his lack of cohesion resembles Esme's schizophrenia by the middle of the novel as "he retire[s] from the image of himself which had stepped down from the mirror above the bar, to dwell apart and watch it move across the room toward the lobby, prepared to applaud this vacant being if things should go well, to abandon it tinted and penniless if things should conspire against it" (512). Like the preternatural portrait in Wilde's *The Picture of Dorian Gray,* the mirror here as elsewhere in *The Recognitions* functions as an occult window on the soul and records with pitiless accuracy the shattering of Otto's identity. After his accident and transformation into "Gordon," the ideal self-who-can-do-more he had sought in so many mirrors, the loss of Otto's sense of self is finalized by the conspicuous absence of all mirrors in his new surroundings, with the exception of the perforated one on the ophthalmoscope Doctor Fell uses to peer into Otto's glazed, empty eyes.

Esther and Esme

A romantic quadrangle links Wyatt and Otto with the novel's two principal female characters, Wyatt's wife Esther, and his model Esme, both of whom tolerate Otto only because of Wyatt's indifference. Both have additional lovers—Esther, Ellery; Esme, Chaby—making Otto even more superfluous, and many of the other male characters seem to have slept with Esther or Esme. But the promiscuity of Greenwich Village women is hardly Gaddis's chief concern. Esther and Esme represent the two traditional forms of female salvation open to the mythic hero, and their inadequacies as suitable anima figures dramatize Gaddis's critique of that very tradition. Though both women share initials and an avocation for writing, they are diametrically opposed: Esther is rational, big-boned, ambitious, and writes prose, while Esme is mystical, delicate, aimless, and writes poetry. Gaddis's prose sharpens the contrast further: his introduction of Esther (78–80) is written in the well-balanced, logically ordered style of Henry James—an author Esther admires—while Esme's equivalent introduction is fractured into two sections (276–77, 298–302) presaging her incipient schizophrenia, and written with the illogic of an interior monologue, punctuated with solipsistic questions and fragments of poems, fictions, and esoteric trivia. They are united, however, in their unrequited love for Wyatt and, after losing him, in their despair.

Esther is the more aggressive of the two. An intelligent woman and a sympathetic character in many ways, Esther is too strongly committed to reason, analysis, intellectual matters, and social success to fulfill the emotional needs of her brooding husband. Complicating matters further, Esther deeply resents being a woman, "and having come to be severely intellectual, probing the past with masculine ruthlessness" (78), she expresses that resentment with a rapacious, castrating sexuality, "seeking, in its clear demand, to absorb the properties which had been withheld from her" (80). Too out of touch with her own femininity, she is hardly in a position to supply the feminine component Wyatt's psyche lacks, and with problems of his own, Wyatt is in no position to help her find herself. Consequently, their marriage is a study in frustration, their temperaments nicely set off by Esther's "thralldom to the perfection of Mozart, work of genius without an instant of hesitation or struggle, genius to which [Wyatt's] argument opposed the heroic struggle constantly rending the music of Beethoven, struggle never resolved and triumphed until the end" (81). Too similar to Aunt May in her schematic outlook on life, Esther loses Wyatt to someone more like his lost mother.

Gretchen to Wyatt's Faust, Esme has been sent to him by the novel's Mephistopheles, Recktall Brown. A promiscuous manic-depressive schizophrenic addicted to heroin, she nevertheless models as the Virgin Mary in Wyatt's religious forgeries ("No needle marks on your Annunciation's arm, now," Brown reminds him [259]), but even outside his studio she is consistently described as resembling a painting (183, 193, 197, 306, 912). With so many keys to character to be found in mirrors and works of art in *The Recognitions,* it is worth noting the difference between the paintings with which Esther and Esme are associated. During his marriage, Wyatt works at restoring "a late eighteenth-century American painting in need of a good deal of work, the portrait of a woman with large bones in her face but an unprominent nose, a picture which looked very much like Esther" (88). Later, turning an ultraviolet light on the restored painting, Wyatt sees another *Dorian Gray*–like revelation of his wife's soul: "in the woman's face, the portions he had restored shone dead black, a face touched with the irregular chiaroscuric hand of lues and the plague, tissues ulcerated under the surface which reappeared in complaisant continence the instant he turned the violet light from it, and upon the form of Esther who had come, looking over his shoulder, and fallen stricken there on the floor without a word" (118). This remarkable passage, with its images from syphilis and disease, not only reveals Wyatt's sexual revulsion from his wife, but more importantly places the blame on Wyatt for Esther's subsequent decline, as though caused by the sympathetic magic of his voodooistic painting.

Esme, on the other hand, is associated with Wyatt's unfinished painting of Camilla, the other virgin of *The Recognitions*. If the spirit of Camilla was translated into the soul of the Barbary ape, Heracles, it finds its present reincarnation in Esme by way of numerous parallels and verbal echoes: Esme is said to have a child four years old (196), the age at which Wyatt realized he had lost his mother; Esme has "a vague look of yearning, but that without expectation" (273), an echo of "the unchanging, ungratified yearning in the face of Camilla on the living-room mantel" (33); before her suicide attempt, Esme dons Camilla's Byzantine earrings with the same bloody results (469–70) as Camilla experienced (14), and after the suicide attempt goes "over to a drawer, looking for something" (480) just as Camilla's ghost had returned after her death to her sewing room, "looking for something" (20); Esme too becomes "an apparition" with a face "delicately intimate in the sharp-boned hollow-eyed virginity of unnatural shadows" (745), restored to a spiritual state of virginity as was Wyatt's ghostly mother before her.

Although Esme is associated with a wide variety of other female figures of salvation in addition to the Virgin Mary and Faust's Gretchen—Dante's Beatrice, Saint Rose of Lima, the Flying Dutchman's Senta, Peer Gynt's Solveig, Lucius's Isis, Saint Francis's Clare, even the king's daughter in the Grimm Brothers' "The Frog King"— she is elsewhere associated with succubae and sirens, and when Wyatt deigns to think of her at all, it is unfortunately in her role as temptress. Rebelling from Brown in his role as the Troll King, Wyatt comes to view Esme more as Ibsen's Green-clad One than as the maternal Solveig and at that point flees from her offer of intimacy to return to his father and take up the priesthood.[6] Given the close association between Esme and Camilla, unconscious fears of incest also seem to be at work in Wyatt's troubled mind. But after the destruction by fire of the *Stabat Mater* modelled on Camilla and Esme—Wyatt having found in Esme's face the lines necessary to complete the old portrait—he realizes the mistake he made in spurning the one woman capable of offering him selfless love. Returning to New York to expose his forgeries and to find Esme, he bungles the first and fails the second, then reluctantly abandons her a final time to travel to Spain and seek out his mother's tomb to do penance.

To some extent, Esme resembles another schizophrenic in American literature, Nicole in Fitzgerald's *Tender Is the Night.* "Nicole, the goddess who failed," Leslie Fiedler has written of her in terms applicable to Esme, "is postulated in the novel as a schizophrenic, in an attempt to explain her double role as Fair Lady and Dark, her two faces, angelic and diabolic, the melting and the grinning mask."[7] Both faces are turned toward Stanley after Wyatt disappears; by day he tries to convert her to his Catholicism, but by night her "simulacra" assail him "immodest in dress and licentious in nakedness, many-limbed as some wild avatar of the Hindu cosmology [. . .] full-breasted and vaunting the belly, limbs indistinguishable until he was brought down between them and stifled in moist collapse" (828). Ever the victim of male projections, Esme slips deeper into madness and religious mania as the novel nears its conclusion, her unrequited love for Wyatt causing her to waste away, "so quickly as though she . . . she had no will to live," as Stanley mournfully confesses, reporting her Firbankian death, a "staphylococcic infection [. . .] from kissing Saint-Peter-in-the-Boat" (953). One of the strangest yet memorable heroines in contemporary literature, Esme betrays the absurdities of the role of romantic redemptress forced upon so many female characters by males who prefer virgins and whores to any more complex woman in between.

Recktall Brown and Basil Valentine

Recktall Brown enters *The Recognitions* by way of the same Satanic invocation Goethe's Faust uses to summon Mephistopheles—both spells based on the medieval *Key of Solomon*—and thereafter is usually seen wreathed in cigar smoke, basking in the infernal heat of his apartment, and surrounded by shadows. With greater relish for Grand Guignol than for subtlety, Gaddis arrays Brown in all the trappings of a twentieth-century devil, a Mammon of the modern world: "—A publisher? A collector? A dealer? Recktall Brown sounded only mildly interested. —People who don't know me, they say a lot of things about me. He laughed then, but the laughter did not leave his throat. —A lot of things. You'd think I was wicked as hell, even if what I do for them turns out good. I'm a business man" (141). Playing upon Wyatt's various frustrations and disappointments, Brown talks Wyatt into forging paintings for him, offering the motto "—Money gives significance to anything" (144) in place of Saint Irenaeus's motto at the beginning of *The Recognitions*, "God gives significance to anything" (as one might loosely translate *"Nihil cavum neque sine signo apud Deum"*). Just as the devil replaces God in Wyatt's world, Brown replaces Rev. Gwyon to a great extent, and thereafter calls him "my boy" and watches over him like a gruff but protective father.

As crass and vulgar as his raunchy name, Recktall Brown nonetheless harbors an ideal "self-who-can-do-more" that he betrayed in his pursuit of material gain. As with the others, that more beautiful self resides in works of art in his possession. One is a portrait of Brown when younger, before which he sometimes stands "with fond veneration" for "the youth he reverenced there" (228). But like the other uncanny paintings and mirrors in the novel, this too is symbolically accurate and unmasks his grasping greed by its disproportionately large hands until, "passing it hundreds of times in the years since, often catching up one hand in the other before him, his hands came to resemble these in the portrait" (228). "Hands like that, on these beautiful things?" Basil Valentine will gloat over Brown's corpse, going on to compare Brown to the Chancellor Rolin in Van Eyck's *Virgin and Child and Donor* (689). But just as Rolin "combined rigid piety with excesses of pride, of avarice and of lust" (in the words of one of Gaddis's sources),[8] Brown does display some appreciation for the beautiful objects he deals in—especially for a set of fifteenth-century Italian armor whose beauty proves his undoing. Early in the novel Brown admits, "It's my favorite thing here" (232), a preference he reiterates at his fatal Christmas Eve party (664). In that same early chapter, Valentine had engaged Wyatt in prescient banter, teasing him with "Brown tells me you have another self. Oh, don't be upset, it's not uncommon you know, not at all uncommon. Why, even Brown has one. That's why he drinks to excess occasionally, trying to slip up on it and grab it. Mark me, he's going to get too close one day, and it's going to turn around and break his neck for him" (253). Drinking to excess the night of the party, knowing Wyatt is no longer under his control and threatening to expose their forgeries, Brown makes a foolish attempt to climb into his beloved armor, which does indeed "break his neck for him" as he falls and clatters down the stairs.

His death, like so many of the deaths in *The Recognitions,* is absurd but symbolically apt; watching him climb into the armor, a visiting member of England's Royal Academy is reminded of an essay he once wrote: "The devil, wearing false calves, do you recall? Mephistopheles, don't you know, in mffft that ponderous thing by Goethe. Good heavens yes, wearing false calves, don't you know, to cover his cloven feet and his mphhht calves, yes. Well my thesis, don't you see, was that these things weren't simply a disguise, to fool people and all that sort of thing, but that some sort of mfft . . . aesthetic need you might say, some sort of nostalgia for beauty, don't you see, he being a fallen angel and all that sort of thing, [. . .]" (676). Bending over the corpse of this fallen angel, "the heavy figure in perfect grace despite its distension hurled down among the roses" of the Aubusson carpet (681), Wyatt weeps for Brown as he does for no other character in the book, in quick succession associating him with the Grimm Brothers' king, *Tosca*'s Cavaradossi, Graves's crucified wren, "old earth," *Peer Gynt*'s Troll King, and finally, however, as a "luxury," the indulgent father who allowed Wyatt to play at Flemish painter for two years and protected him from the outside world.

Despite his corrupt dealings, Brown admired Wyatt and had his best interests at heart. "I want to watch out for you," he once said with gruff sincerity (365). Not so his partner Basil Valentine, who appears at first to be more sensitive to Wyatt's difficulties but who later exposes himself to be as predatory as Esther. Like Wyatt's wife, Valentine is aligned with reason and analysis, and is likewise envious of Wyatt's abilities. "He's jealous of you, my boy, can't you see that?" Brown warns him (364), but Wyatt is initially seduced by the companionship of one whose learning and aesthetic tastes match his own. Viewing Wyatt's forgery of a van der Goes *Death of the Virgin,* Valentine murmurs, "The simplicity . . . it's the way I would paint" (334). Disturbed later by the damage Wyatt inflicts upon the face in this painting, Valentine surreptitiously restores the face himself (with results Wyatt finds laughably vulgar), perhaps from the same "nostalgia for beauty" the British R.A. spoke of, perhaps from his vain desire to participate in Wyatt's artistry: "Because you're . . . part of me . . . damn you" (692). Wyatt stabs him at that point and leaves him for dead, sensing enough truth in Valentine's words to want to kill that part of him epitomized by the haughty aesthete.

Graced with taste, intelligence, and "the best education money can buy" (364), Valentine uses these gifts to place as much distance as possible between himself and others, specifically "the stupid, thick-handed people, [. . .] whose idea of necessity is paying the gas bill, the masses who as their radios assure them, are under no obligation" (386). Valentine insists on obligations to church, state, culture, tradition. Consequently, he is involved (in addition to Brown's art scam) in shipping works of art "back to Europe" where they "belong" (688–89), working to restore the Hapsburg monarchy to Hungary, and acting in the clandestine interests of the Jesuits—activities that make up the novel's murky espionage subplot but that have in common an attempt to turn back the clock to an age of aristocratic privilege when the masses knew their place and kept their hands off art. Making his acquaintance late in the novel, Esme calls him the Cold Man and challenges him, "But why do you do the things you do? Why do you live the life you live?" (923). Valentine defends his reactionary politics with an appeal to the same kind of aesthetic elitism that led Pound and Eliot (among others) to favor authoritarian governments: "because any sanctuary of power . . . protects beautiful things. To keep people . . . to control people, to give them something . . . anything cheap that will satisfy them at the moment, to keep them away from beautiful things, to keep them where their hands can't touch beautiful things, their hands that . . . touch and defile and . . . and break beautiful things, hands that hate beautiful things, and fear beautiful things, and touch and defile and fear and break beautiful things" (924). To achieve this end, Valentine is willing to forsake all humane obligations, going so far as to arrange for the assassination of his childhood friend Martin. Invited to join Valentine in this sterile ivory tower, Wyatt stabs him and flees from New York, immersing himself for the next few months in the simple arts of the people.

In the novel's religious scheme, Valentine is associated not only with Catholicism but with Gnosticism, that early Christian heresy that held matter to be evil and urged nonparticipation in a fallen world. In his notes, Gaddis wrote: "Basil Valentine, who is the gnostic presumption [. . .] is finally stricken down with insomnia, for his very refusal to realize and grant the worth of matter, that is, of other people. The essence of his gnosticism is largely an implacable hatred for matter. It is that element of aescetecism [sic] common in so many religious expressions turned, not upon the self, but upon humanity."[9] In a kind of parody of Agatha of the Cross—"the saint who didn't sleep for the last eight years of her life" (365)—Valentine survives Wyatt's attack only to lapse into an insomnia for which his Hungarian doctors can find no "reason," and finally expires babbling Latin, which exposes the failure of his kind of Gnosticism: the penultimate word in his quotation "Aut castus sit aut pereat" (Be pure *or* perish) becomes "et pereat" (*and* perish) (949)—suggesting that any withdrawal to a pure realm of thought without the "impurity" of human relations will lead to sterility at best (note Valentine's homosexuality), and at worst to death.

Stanley and Anselm

That same Latin motto can be said to govern the life of Stanley, who likewise perishes from a mistaken notion of purity, a mistake for which he is taunted throughout the novel by his friend Anselm. In the novel's religious dialectic, Stanley and Anselm represent the two extremes of institutional Catholicism and primitive Christianity, respectively, both making explicit in their arguments some of the tensions implicit in Wyatt's religious conflicts. Raised a Protestant but drawn in his extremity to the priesthood of Stanley's church, Wyatt will finally settle for Saint Augustine's simple injunction "Love, and do what you want to" (899). But Wyatt's movement from one to the other—with excursions into Calvinism, satanism, mystical alchemy, and paganism—owes much of its theological depth to the religious debates held by Stanley and Anselm in their various Greenwich Village haunts.

Neither ever meets Wyatt, yet both are linked to him by numerous metonymic gestures, relations, and attitudes: both Stanley and Anselm know and love Esme (in their respective ways); both are artists—Stanley a composer, Anselm a poet—and Stanley especially shares Wyatt's religious obsession with authentic art and his preference for working at night; Stanley's eyes burn green in moments of anger as Wyatt's do, and he apparently lives only a block north of Wyatt's Horatio Street studio; Anselm has Wyatt's distrust of rationality and comes into possession of Wyatt's father's razor, with unmanning results; and the three of them, as Max points out, are "all mothers' sons" (534) suffering from the psychological tensions between mothers and sons, between Mother Church and her wayward children.

Reminiscent of Dostoyevski's Prince Myshkin or Alyosha Karamazov, Stanley is the holy fool of *The Recognitions,* moving through its sordid scenes with unassailable purity and goodwill. But while Dostoyevski's saintly characters are blessed with some degree of serenity, Stanley has an air of gloom and uneasiness about him. "A candid look of guilt hung about him" we are told at his first appearance (182), standing forlorn at a party attended by the three women who will assail that purity he so zealously guards: Agnes Deigh, a lapsed Catholic he hopes to bring back into the fold; Hannah, a dumpy Village artist hopelessly in love with him; and Esme, his spiritual sister in many ways, whom he wants to "save" but who inspires in him feelings closer to eros than agape. In addition, Stanley is haunted by the thought of his mother, moribund in a nearby hospital, and his unfinished organ mass, which he hopes to complete before her death, but which proves to be quite literally the death of him.

Stanley shares Wyatt's frustrations with creating sacred art in such profane times, and most of his aesthetic pronouncements could as easily come from Wyatt's lips (cf. 186 with 89, 616 with 113–14). But he also shares Wyatt's self-isolation and discomfort with human contact, a terror of intimacy that approaches cold-heartedness at times. Instinctively recoiling from the first of Agnes's many loving gestures, "the consecrated mind thrust the vagrant heart aside" (193), a stance he maintains throughout the novel, all the while insisting that love and unity can still be found in the Church. Disturbed by "the gulf between people and modern art" (632), Stanley composes music in the Renaissance style of the Gabrielis and loses himself in nostalgia for those ages past when art and religion went hand in hand to bind communities together—much as Wyatt imagines fifteenth-century Flanders. He quietly opposes the easy cynicism of Max, Otto, and the others until Anselm, for one, can stand it no longer. Flinging Matthew 10:35–36 in Stanley's face ("For I am come to set man at variance [. . .]"), Anselm hisses, "Yes, there's your gulf, the hand of your everlasting Christ!" (632), then goes on to attack Stanley's confidence in "spiritual love" with sputtering anger:

—And stop this damned . . . this God-damned sanctimonious attitude, he cried, twisting free, and they stood face to face. —Stanley, by Christ Stanley that's what it is, and you go around accusing people of refusing to humble themselves and submit to the love of Christ and you're the one, you're the one who refuses love, you're the one all the time who can't face it, who can't face loving, and being loved right here, right in this lousy world, this God-damned world where you are right now, right . . . right now. (635)

Finally taunting him with a pornographic photograph of Esme, he pinpoints Stanley's real fear, that of sexual intimacy, the repression that will return to haunt Stanley during his ocean voyage with Esme.

Anselm challenges the fastidious, rather austere Christianity of Eliot (whose works Stanley can quote) in the spirit of Yeats's Crazy Jane, who spurns her bishop's "heavenly mansions" because she knows better that "Love has pitched his mansion in / The place of excrement."[10] Concealing Tolstoy's *Kingdom of God* within a girlie magazine, more blasphemous than pious, Anselm is an enemy not of the religious but of the religiose. He recognizes the New Testament for the radical document it is and is contemptuous of those who compromise or prettify its stringent call for humility and renunciation, a call he feels others should struggle with as intensely as he does. "Work out your own salvation with fear and trembling" Saint Paul counsels (Phil. 2:12), not with the cheerful confidence so many Christians exude. After his friend Charles attempts suicide, only to be abandoned by his mother because he won't return to Grand Rapids and submit to Christian Science, Anselm turns on Hannah:

—It's the complacency I can't stand, Anselm burst out. —I can't stand it anywhere, but most of all I can't stand it in religion. Did you see Charles' mother? did you see her smile? that holier-than-thou Christian smile, [. . .] I don't blame Charles a God damn bit for flipping. God is Love! We'd all flip, taking that from your own mother and you're lying there with your wrists slashed open. But love on this earth? Christ! . . . pity? compassion? That's why I've got my balls in an uproar if you want to know, talking about some kind of love floating around Christ knows where, but what did she give him? When he wouldn't go back to Grand fucking Rapids and be treated by Christian Science? She gave him one of those eternally damned holier-than-thou smiles and left him here. She left him here without a cent, to let Bellevue kill him, or let him try it again himself. God is Love, for Christ sake! If Peter had smiled like a Christian Scientist Christ would have kicked his teeth down his throat. (531–32)

One moment quipping "I envy Christ, he had a disease named after him" (534), the next moment proving the existence of God with citations from Saints Augustine and Anselm (for whom he abandoned his given name Arthur) and tearing to shreds someone's beatnik version of the Paternoster (536), Anselm veers violently between fierce blasphemy and a grudging respect for Christ's teachings. As sensual as Stanley is chaste, however, Anselm cannot accommodate Christianity's opposition to sex: "With all the . . . rotten betrayals around us, and that, that . . . that one moment of trust, is sin?" (526). But the sexual encounters he boasts of are acts of victimization, not trust, and may be a reaction against the apparent homosexual attraction to both Charles and Stanley that he throttles throughout the book. Unshaven, broke, his problems are compounded by frequent drunkenness and the rejection (by publisher Recktall Brown) of his religious poetry. He is the angriest character in this angry novel.

"Why do you fight it so hard?" (633) Stanley asks him, echoing Esther to Wyatt (118). Anselm shares with Wyatt and Stanley an incapacity for tenderness and, more important, a problematic relation to his mother. Anselm describes her as a religious fanatic who is more interested in dogs than in her troubled son—which accounts for his habit of crawling on all fours from time to time. It is after a hallucinatory encounter with his mother in a subway that Anselm castrates himself with the Reverend Gwyon's old razor, stolen while he was at Esther's party, in emulation of "Origen, that most extraordinary Father of the Church, whose third-century enthusiasm led him to castrate himself so that he might repeat the *hoc est corpus meum, Dominus,* without the distracting interference of the rearing shadow of the flesh" (103).

As "screwed up with religion" as Stanley is (182), Anselm follows in Thomas Merton's footsteps and retreats to a monastery out West to write his memoirs, much to Stanley's amazement.[11] Stanley doesn't fare as well; as unworldly as Esme, he too perishes in the highly symbolic conclusion. In the last two pages of the novel, Gaddis evokes in compressed form all of the major tensions in *The Recognitions:* appearance vs. reality (the church at Fenestrula is smaller than it looked at night); the ideal vs. the real ("there was nothing, absolutely nothing, the way it should be"); shadowy night vs. "the vast consciousness of the lighted sky"; American innocence vs. European worldliness (Stanley is dressed in red, white, and blue, playing an oversized organ donated by an American, and is unable to comprehend the Italian priest's warnings); the demands of art vs. the need for love; human loss vs. artistic gain; the Church as "a private chapel" vs. "a public convenience" (both the same building, Stanley realizes); and religion as a refuge vs. a tomb. Church bells ring in a new life for Wyatt (and possibly for Otto and Anselm), but they toll the impending death of the novel's most devout Catholic and most devoted artist, a martyr to both art and religion, "for the work required it" (956).

Frank Sinisterra and Mr. Pivner

There are nearly as many fathers seeking sons in *The Recognitions* as sons fleeing mothers in search of spiritual fathers. No one in the novel confuses his mother with anyone else's—"*Amor matris,* subjective and objective genitive, may be the only true thing in life," as Stephen Dedalus suggests[12]—but a number of skewed father and son combinations link the older generation with the younger. Rev. Gwyon abandons his son first for the Son, then for the Sun; thus abandoned, Wyatt is taken up by father figures as diverse as Recktall Brown, Basil Valentine, Frank Sinisterra, the novelist Ludy, and the porter at the monastery where he ends up; Sinisterra, the natural but disappointed father of Chaby, is mistaken by Otto for his own father before becoming a father figure to Wyatt; Otto's father, Mr. Pivner, misses his own son but finds one in Eddie Zefnic; Stanley briefly enjoys a father figure in Father Martin; Arnie Munk fails at becoming a father so regularly that his wife steals a baby in desperation, while the homosexual Big Anna the Swede becomes a legal father "because the only way I can possibly get *hold* of little Giono is to a*dopt* him" (825); and even our Father Who art in heaven emerges as little more than a useful fiction, anybody's or nobody's father.

Frank Sinisterra, another of Gaddis's great comic creations, is as devout a Catholic as Stanley and as devoted an artist as Wyatt; he plays key roles both in directing Wyatt's life and in clarifying his aesthetics. Introduced wearing the first of many disguises, Sinisterra poses as ship's surgeon on the *Purdue Victory* and puts an end to Camilla's life during an improvised appendectomy. Apprehended and sentenced to prison—which he resents "no more than Saint Augustine resented the withdrawal he had made from the world when living near Tagaste" (488)—Sinisterra does not reappear until nearly five hundred pages later, but thereafter plays an increasingly important role first in Otto's then in Wyatt's life.

Later masquerading as Mr. Yák, he runs into Wyatt at Camilla's tomb in Spain and takes him under his wing, first because he sees this as an opportunity to make restitution for his earlier misdeed, and second because he finds in Wyatt the son he never had in Chaby. Despite all his fatherly efforts, Sinisterra has not been able to prevent his real son from becoming a "bum":

—Whenever I was home to give him the benefit of my study and experience, I tried to teach him. I taught him how to spring a Yale lock with a strip of celluloid. I taught him how to open a lock with wet thread and a splinter. I taught him how to look like he has a deformed spine, or a deformed foot. Nobody taught me all that. I learned it myself. It was a lot of work, and he had me right there to teach him, right here, his own father. So what does he learn? Nothing. He's never done a day's work in his life. You think a bum like that I'd claim him for my son? (493)

But he knows Wyatt is no "bum," as he often tells him, and he swells with paternal pride when he learns that Wyatt knows enough about Egyptian mummies to help him with his most ambitious counterfeit. Sinisterra re-christens Wyatt with the name Camilla intended for him, and by the time "Mr. Yák," "Stephan," and their "mummy" settle onto a train, they resemble "a weary and not quite respectable family" (812).

Sinisterra takes Rev. Gwyon's place by quite literally following in his footsteps: his approach to San Zwingli (776) contains numerous verbal echoes of Gwyon's earlier approach (16), and both share the "glittering eye" of Coleridge's Ancient Mariner (428, 794). Both watch the rain from the windows of their Madrid rooms and are chilled by the thought of leaving a window open or "something precious left out in the rain" (12, 821). Sinisterra has "a light in his eye seldom seen today but in asylums and occasional pulpits" (776), Rev. Gwyon's current and former location. But more importantly, Sinisterra provides Wyatt with the moral instruction his deranged father was incapable of giving: he sees Wyatt through his difficult symbolic death by water (a feverish delirium), and in their last conversation, as Wyatt/Stephan searches his face "as though waiting for some answer from him," Sinisterra counsels, "—What you'd want to do maybe, he commenced, —you might like to go to a monastery awhile, you don't have to turn into a monk, you are like a guest there" (816–17). Stephen follows his advice and there experiences the hillside epiphany that frees him into a new life.

Like Stanley, Sinisterra dies a martyr to his art and is likewise guilty of hoarding all his love for his work (817). A parody of a genuine artist, Sinisterra lavishes on his counterfeiting projects all his technique and expertise, and "like any sensitive artist caught in the toils of unsympathetic critics" smarts from unkind reviews (5–6). A comic voice in the novel's aesthetic debate, Sinisterra exemplifies the danger of overreliance on heartless virtuosity; while Wyatt is struck by the beauty of the Dama de Elche on a Spanish one-peseta note, Sinisterra dismisses it as "A cheap engraving job" (782). As Stanley insists, "It isn't for love of the thing itself that an artist works, but so that through it he's expressing love for something higher, because that's the only place art is really free, serving something higher than itself" (632). Sinisterra works only for laundered cash, and his "art" is of course limited to slavish imitation with an intent to defraud, not to enlighten or to serve anything higher. Sinisterra studies and respects the "old masters" (519) as reverently as Stanley or Wyatt, but erroneously considers "a crafts-man, an artist" to be interchangeable terms (785), blind to the motives that elevate a craftsman to an artist. His career provides a ludicrous but illuminating dimension to the novel's consideration of the artist's role in society and the aesthetics that distinguish artistry from mere craftsmanship.

Neither artist nor craftsman, Mr. Pivner is the most conventional character in *The Recognitions,* living a life of quiet desperation in the Age of Anxiety, practically a case study out of Riesman's *The Lonely Crowd* (1950). Trusting "there would be time" (292), Pivner has all of Prufrock's doubts and misgivings but none of his romantic longings, and like Eliot's dreamer he shrinks from asserting himself in any but the meekest way. Although he makes only a half-dozen appearances in the novel—each one a quiet vignette expertly poised between pathos and bathos—Pivner performs two important functions: first, he ex-emplifies the numbing conventional life Gaddis's more unconventional characters are reacting against; and second, he provides a mundane counterpart to the more exotic search for meaning and authenticity conducted by the others.

As Rev. Gwyon has his books on myth and magic, Wyatt his al-chemical tracts, Esme her Rilke, Stanley Eliot, Anselm Saint Anselm, Valentine Tertullian, and Sinisterra Bicknall's *Counterfeit Detector* for 1839, Mr. Pivner has Dale Carnegie. He studies *How to Win Friends and Influence People* with the same attention the others spend on their authors, although to his credit Pivner is more interested in winning friends than influencing people—especially the friendship of his es-tranged son Otto. Carnegie's call for "a new way of life" (498) is a profane version of the more sacred calls made by Christ, Dante, and Rilke to which the other characters are striving to respond. Although Pivner is largely unaware that he and Carnegie's millions of other read-ers vainly pursue "the Self which had ceased to exist the day they stopped seeking it alone" (286), he, too, has moments of recognition, glimpses of the "self-who-can-do-more." He is generally made nervous by such music as Mendelssohn's Reformation Symphony, for example, "but sometimes he was struck with a bar of 'classical' music, a series of chords such as these which poured forth now, a sense of loneliness and confirmation together, a sense of something lost, and a sense of recognition which he did not understand" (501). His fleeting impulses toward authenticity are conveyed with the same complex of alchemical/metallurgical/counterfeit imagery Gaddis uses throughout the novel: "the strain of perfect metal in his alloy cried out for perfection," but under a relentless barrage of meretricious advertising, flattering self-help books, and the glib assurances of science and reason, "that perfect particle was submerged, again satisfied with any counterfeit of itself which would represent its worth amongst others" (293). While others in the novel rage against the dying of the lights of civilization, Pivner goes gentle into that benighted modern world.

Pivner is arrested while listening with his surrogate son Eddie Zefnic to the famous aria from Handel's *Messiah* that begins, "He was despiséd, rejected, a man of sorrows and acquainted with grief" (743) and is later duly "crucified" with a frontal lobotomy (at Eddie's suggestion, who joins the novel's ranks of Oedipal headhunters) after being sent to prison as a counterfeiter—on the slimmest of evidence, it should be noted, however appropriate the metaphor. (We recall that one of the headlines Pivner had read earlier in the novel was "Lobotomy to Cure Man of Writing Dud Checks" [289].) The sense behind this outlandish turn of events is that Pivner is a victim of the same kind of anxiety neurosis that budding scientist Eddie Zefnic eagerly observes being inflicted experimentally upon "a whole bunch of kids (ha ha I mean little goats)," he writes, "which are hooked up so that when the light dims it gets a shock, so after a while then the minute the light dims the kid backs into the corner and gets tense but then we change the signals around on him then he gets the real anxiety neurosis" (933). The makers of postwar society have changed the signals around to the point where old values and certainties seem no longer appropriate, and new ones intent only on bringing "a good price in the market place" (502). Those like Pivner without the strength to maintain the old values or without the courage to light out for new territory may as well agree to a lobotomy and have done with it.

At the quiet center of the novel, Mr. Pivner is Gaddis's Willy Loman, and his failure is a similar tragedy for the common man. He struggles to maintain values that seem curiously unreal in the brave new world of "the Age of Publicity" (736), values at odds with those of the unctuous radio announcers he listens to so politely: "What was this anomaly in him, that still told him that the human voice is to be listened to? the printed word to be read? What was this expectant look, if it was not hope? this attentive weariness, if it was not faith? this bewildered failure to damn, if it was not charity?" (502). Amidst the angst-ridden quests for philosophers' stones and the will of God by the wild-eyed characters in the novel, Mr. Pivner's failed quest for love and authenticity is blandly undramatic, and perhaps for that very reason all the more tragic.

Baedeker's *Babel*

Among the other characters in this well-populated novel is a young writer named Willie working on a novel called "Baedeker's *Babel*," to be based on the Clementine *Recognitions*. Gaddis's own novel is a kind of Baedeker's guide to the Babel of modern civilization and to the varieties of babble its citizens speak. "The decay of overripe forms of civilization is as suggestive a spectacle as the growth of new ones," Huizinga writes of fifteenth-century Flanders,[13] and in that spirit Gaddis aligns mid-century America not only with Van Eyck's Flanders— "a world where everything was done for the same reasons everything's done now [. . .] for vanity and avarice and lust" (689–90)—but with "Caligula's Rome, with a new circus of vulgar bestialized suffering in the newspapers every morning" (386), and even with Ikhnaton's Egypt, as the British R. A. obligingly explains: "Too much gold, that was their difficulty, gold kicking around all over the place, and vulgarity everywhere, eh? Yes, that's what happens, that's when the decadence sets in, eh? Same damn thing running around today from the look of things, eh? Wasn't like this fifty years ago, eh? Good heavens no, people then who had money inherited it don't you know, knew how to spend it. Some sense of responsibility to their culture, eh?" (658).

This trans-cultural historical approach is similar to that used in *The Waste Land*. Like Eliot, Gaddis dramatizes "the world of fire" (726) kindled by those for whom vanity, avarice, and lust have obliterated any sense of responsibility to their culture, much less to their god. There is indeed what one critic called "an odor of spoilt culture" hanging over *The Recognitions*,[14] a stench given off by those for whom learning has deteriorated to fodder for cocktail party chat:

—Einstein . . . someone said.
—Epstein . . . said someone else.
—Gertrude . . .
—Of course you're familiar with Heisenberg's Principle of Uncertainty. Have you ever observed sand fleas? Well I'm working on a film which not

only substantiates it but illustrates perfectly the metaphor of the theoretic and the real situation. And after all, what else *is* there?
　—Who *was* it that said, "a little lower than the angels"?
　—That? it's in that poem about "What is man, that thou art mindful of him." That was Pope.
　—Which one? (600)[15]

It is not surprising, then, that the novel's most sympathetic characters—and the ones who offer Wyatt the best advice—are the mad, the uneducated, the disenfranchised: Janet, the Town Carpenter, Esther's sister Rose (all of whom are deranged to some degree), Fuller, the peasant girl Pastora, and the old porter at the Real Monasterio. When Wyatt boasts he can lock out the world, it is Fuller who tells him, "Seem like such a measure serve no good purpose, sar. Then the mahn lose everything he suppose to keep, and keep everything he suppose to lose" (347). It is Janet who defines damnation more succinctly than any church father and who reminds Wyatt, "No love is lost" (442). And it is the porter who will not allow Wyatt to lock out the world any longer by staying in a monastery. "Go where you're wanted," he tells him (894), sending him back to Pastora. *The Recognitions* is not a repudiation of education or culture, of course, but an attack on its misuse by those who come and go speaking of "the solids in Uccello" and other matters with little or no understanding, counterfeiters of the intellect who drop names and botch quotations in their desperate attempts to win friends and influence people.
　These characters have a weary apologist in Agnes Deigh, whose extraordinary 3500-word suicide note (757–63) delineates with nerve-shattered lyricism the complex difficulties and risks involved in allowing anyone a glimpse of the private self hiding behind that protective coloring of culture. "Before the flowers of friendship faded friendship faded," she writes (quoting Gertrude Stein, in whose style the letter is couched), and so Agnes and her flock skip over friendship and its perils and simply exchange the "flowers" of friendship—that is, empty civilities that counterfeit sincere friendship, exchanged "in ritual denial of the ripe knowledge that we are drawing away from one another, that we share only one thing, share the fear of belonging to another, or to others, or to God" (103). Here Gaddis quotes from Eliot's "East Coker," but the world he dramatizes in his novel is the spiritually bankrupt one of *The Waste Land,* and like the poet before him Gaddis weighs an entire civilization in the balance and finds it wanting.

Chapter Four

J R: What America Is All About

"We live in a country that never grew up," Gaddis has Hannah complain in *The Recognitions* (748), and it is fitting that his second novel—a comic exposé of "what America is all about," as one of its refrains goes—should be named after an eleven-year-old boy who epitomizes a society where stock options "mature" more regularly than people do, and where trucks drive by emblazoned with the slogan "None of us grew but the business."[1] Just as everyone in the counterfeit world of *The Recognitions* moves in relation to Wyatt, everyone in the paper world of *J R* moves in relation to J R Vansant, a slovenly but clever boy who transforms a small "portforlio" of mail-order acquisitions and penny stocks into an unwieldy financial empire, bringing the economy to the brink of ruin simply by dedicating himself with a vengeance to "the traditional ideas and values that have made America what it is today" (652). "I mean like remember this here book that time where they wanted me to write about success and like free enterprise and all hey?" J R asks through a dangling telephone on the last page of the novel. In *J R* we have one of the most searching analyses of "success and like free enterprise" in American literature and one of the funniest and most scathing critiques of those traditional ideas and values.

Money Talks

The most radical feature of *J R* is its narrative mode: except for an occasional transitional passage in elliptical prose, the novel is composed entirely of dialogue—726 pages of voices without a single chapter break or sectional space. Novels written primarily in dialogue have been done before—for example, by Ronald Firbank (whom Gaddis has read) and Ivy Compton-Burnett (whom he hasn't)—but never to the extreme lengths Gaddis takes it. To make matters more difficult, his dialogue is not the literary dialogue of most novels, with completed grammatical sentences helpfully larded with *she said*s and explanatory asides by the author on what the characters actually mean by what they say. Instead, *J R* reads like a transcript of real speech: ungrammatical, often truncated, with constant interruptions by other characters (and by telephones, televisions, and radios), with rarely an identifying (and never an interpretive) remark by the author.

"It is the thesis" of Norbert Wiener's *The Human Use of Human Beings,* an important source of ideas for *J R,* "that society can only be understood through a study of the messages and communication facilities which belong to it,"[2] a thesis that Gaddis puts to the test by casting the entire novel in dialogue—a narrative mode that puts readers to the test as well. Such a mode makes extraordinary demands upon a reader; it demands active involvement and concentration on the reader's part, not passivity. (This point seems unnecessary until one looks at Gaddis's reviews; "Relax your attention for a single paragraph," one reviewer complained, "and you've missed something crucial, and must reread"—as though a better novelist would make allowances for daydreaming.[3]) Jack Gibbs, a major character, pinpoints this problem during a drunken conversation with Edward Bast, a young composer: "problem most God damned readers rather be at the movies. Pay attention here bring something to it take something away problem most God damned writing's written for readers perfectly happy who they are rather be at the movies, come in empty-handed go out the same God damned way what I told him Bast. Ask them to bring one God damned bit of effort want everything done for them they get up and go to the movies" (289–90). That "pay attention here" is directed to the reader as much as to Bast; while any text benefits more from an active reading than a passive one, *J R* leaves the reader no choice. The passive reader will not last a dozen pages.

The purpose is not to put readers off but to force them to participate in the fiction. Just as radio audiences must use their imaginations more than movie audiences do, Gaddis's readers must join him in creating this fictional world. Noting Gaddis's reliance on one-sided telephone conversations, Carl Malmgren has pointed out that "the telephone conversation becomes an important metaphor *in* and *for* the novel [. . .]: the text of *J R* presents readers with one-half of a phone conversation; they must supply the other half if their experience is to have meaning or coherence. Gaddis's point, of course, is that meaning and coherence are less properties of a text than they are products of activities performed upon it. *J R* takes a form which necessarily demands and fosters

these activities."[4] In this way, the reader's search for meaning and coherence parallels that of the novel's characters—for meaning and coherence are less properties of life than products of activities performed
upon it—and as the attentive reader grows more and more giddy trying
to keep track of the complications of the plot, he or she comes to
experience the same degree of exasperation that Bast, Gibbs, and the
others feel.

Given the novel's great length, it may not be immediately apparent
how lean and economical Gaddis's novel actually is: a more conventional rendering of the same material would easily run twice as long.
In his perceptive review, novelist D. Keith Mano cited a trivial exchange between Stella and Gibbs:

—Do we need the radio?
—Looking for the God damned lighter. (349)

"Yet note that it describes the action," he points out, "while underlining his drunkenness, her arch prose. You'd need four narrative
sentences to accomplish as much. Despite its length, *J R* is a condensation."[5] This point is more apparent when comparing the opening
pages of the novel that appeared as "J. R. or the Boy Inside" (*Dutton
Review,* 1970) with pages 3–44 of the published book. They appear
more or less identical, yet a textual collation reveals that of the six
hundred or so changes Gaddis made, most were deletions, from superfluous punctuation to excess verbiage and most speaker identifications.
The dialogue in the book version is usually more elliptical—making it
harder to follow at times—but greater in verisimilitude and quicker in
narrative pacing. Of course any comparison with a literal transcript of
people speaking—see Andy Warhol's tape-recorded "novel" *a* (1968),
for example—will reveal that Gaddis's characters speak with more variety, wit, and color than their real-life counterparts would. Gaddis's
real achievement lies in his ability to simulate vernacular speech close
enough to insure accuracy while avoiding its shortcomings.

Finally, the exclusive use of dialogue adds to the novel's dramatic
vitality by closing the traditional gap between story-time and text-
time, that is, between the amount of time an episode covers and the
time it takes to read that episode. Shlomith Rimmon–Kenan writes
that "a hypothetical 'norm' of complete correspondence between the
two is only rarely realized,"[6] but most of *J R* maintains this correspondence. Never does Gaddis stop the narrative flow to indulge in a flash-

back or to examine a character's motives, or move things forward with such temporal leapfrogging as "A week later . . . " From Coen's opening query "Money . . . ?" to J R's final "Hey? You listening . . .?" every day in the narrative is tracked by a sleepless narrative eye that pauses only when the characters sleep. (The ideal reader would rest only at those rare junctures: e.g., 75, 155, 234, 316, 414, 491, 580, 669.) As a result, the text quickly builds an irresistible momentum that functions as a formal analogue to the rapid growth of J R's family of companies. By the time Bast cries out, "No now stop, just stop for a minute! This, this whole thing has to stop somewhere don't you understand that?" (298), there is a relentless inevitability driving both J R's enterprises and *J R* itself that makes stopping at that point commercially and aesthetically unthinkable.

A Story of Wall Street

Although its form and intricate convolutions are radical, *J R*'s story material is fairly traditional. It can be separated into five interwoven strands; given the wonderful complexity of the plot, these should be itemized:

1. An interfamilial dispute comes to a head with the death intestate of Thomas Bast, owner of the General Roll Company, and his survivors grapple with future ownership of the company (which may need to go public to finance the substantial death taxes). Half of Thomas's forty-five shares in the company will be inherited by his daughter Stella, and with her husband Norman Angel's twenty-three shares they hope to approach controlling interest in the company. But they face a challenge by the impending return of Thomas's brother James, a composer and conductor, whose share of stock, combined with the twenty-seven shares belonging to his maiden sisters Anne and Julia, will give him close to controlling interest. There are two wild cards: Edward Bast, the illegitimate son of James and Nellie (Thomas's second wife), who may be in a position to claim half of the shares Stella is expecting, thus tilting the balance toward James's ownership; and Jack Gibbs, Stella's former lover, once given five shares for helping the company out. Intent on gaining full control, scheming Stella sets out to prevent Edward from pressing his claim, to learn the location of Gibbs's shares, and perhaps even to wrest Norman's shares away from him. She is successful enough to emerge at the end of the novel with controlling interest in the company—her husband comatose in a hospital from an attempt at suicide.

2. The upper middle-class Bast family dispute out on Long Island has its upper-class counterpart in the Moncrieff family dispute in Manhattan. The former Amy Moncrieff has a bad marriage with Lucien Joubert, a Swiss fortune hunter attracted less by Amy's stunning beauty than by her father Monty Moncrieff's company Typhon International, ruthlessly run by Amy's great-uncle Governor John ("Black Jack") Cates. Typhon owns many of the other companies mentioned in the novel—Diamond Cable, Nobili Pharmaceuticals, Endo Appliance—and has many of its assets tied up in two foundations, one in Amy's name, the other in her son Francis's. A substantial number of shares in Diamond Cable belong to Boody Selk, the jet-setting teen-aged daughter of obnoxious Zona Selk—an old friend of the family—and just as controlling interest in General Roll falls to Stella, controlling interest in Typhon comes into the hands of Amy and Boody by the novel's end.

3. Amy Joubert, Edward Bast, and Jack Gibbs all teach at a junior high school on Long Island, whose principal, Mr. Whiteback (also president of a local bank: he'll give up one or the other "when I know which of them is going to survive" [340–41]), spends most of his time trying to mollify irate members of the board of education such as Major Hyde (an employee of Typhon's Endo Appliance), superintendent Vern Teakell, local politicians and contractors (all with Italian surnames), the right-wing Citizens Union on Neighborhood Teaching ("All women?" Gibbs asks [241]), and visitors from a foundation investigating the disastrous results of the school's adoption of the latest educational technologies.

4. Attending this appalling school is J R Vansant, whose best friend, the nameless son of Major Hyde, shares his interest in writing away for and trading junk mail flyers and career solicitations. "See them in there together getting their mail you suddenly know what the industrial military complex is all about," as Gibbs notes (497). J R's enthusiasm for tacky business opportunities is matched by the Hyde boy's mindless patriotism ("a martial miniature" [33] of his fatuous father), but J R's greater daring launches him on a career that parodies the Horatio Alger paradigm and demonstrates, as Richard Bulliet has written, "that 'the market' so beloved of economic theorists can be convincingly allegorized as an ethically innocent and none-too-bright sixth-grader."[7] Using money from one small venture to finance a slightly larger one, borrowing against that for yet a larger one, J R quickly finds himself the unexpected father of the J R Family of Companies with his grubby fingers in nearly every aspect of the American economy, including the

Basts' General Roll and the Moncrieffs' various companies. (Conveni-
ent summaries of J R's acquisitions can be found on pp. 431, 529–30,
and 656.) His paper empire collapses like a house of cards by the end
of the novel, but he emerges unscathed and bursting with new ideas.

5. Trying their best to skirt the edges of all these business deals and
family disputes are five artists engaged in desperate attempts to keep
their heads clear enough to create art for an indifferent society. As
Gibbs tries to find the motivation to revive his work in progress of
sixteen years, *Agapē Agape* ("a book about order and disorder more of
a, sort of a social history of mechanization and the arts, the destructive
element" [244]), his friend Thomas Eigen tries to finish a play about
the Civil War amidst the distractions of his enervating public relations
work for Typhon and his disintegrating marriage. From Gibbs and
Eigen the reader learns of the struggles of another writer named
Schramm, blocked in his attempts to write about his traumatic World
War II experiences, and of a painter named Schepperman, whose work
is warehoused in Zona Selk's country house to his immense frustration.
A generation younger but facing many of the same obstacles is Edward
Bast, recently graduated from a music conservatory, who reluctantly
agrees to act as J R's "business representive" (as his card reads) in order
to find enough time and money to finish an operatic suite based on
Tennyson's "Locksley Hall" that enshrines his unrequited love for his
cousin Stella, a work later modified to a cantata and finally abandoned
in favor of a piece for unaccompanied cello, written in crayon.

Despite the absence of formal division markers, the novel falls
roughly into thirds, with each third doubling the pace and complications of Gaddis's pentahedral plot. *J R* begins with a society on edge:
the stock market is troubled; Thomas's death has renewed the Bast
family conflict; Edward Bast, Gibbs, and Eigen are feeling the pressures of their respective jobs; every marriage is on the brink; Amy fears
her estranged husband will abduct their son, while her father is more
worried that the press will learn of the conflict in interests that jeo-
pardizes his new government post; and tempers are flaring at J R's
school over an impending teachers' strike and the possible loss of foundation funding. These and many other conflicts come to a boil a third
of the way through the novel on the long Friday that occupies pages
234–86: Schramm commits suicide, Marion tells Gibbs she's leaving
Eigen, Schepperman tries to prevent Zona Selk from removing his
painting from Typhon's lobby, J R has his company off and running
after bringing a minority suit against Diamond Cable for Moncrieff's

transgression of a company by-law (settling out of court for damages based on 100 times holdings), and Bast finds himself reluctantly stuck with a position as an executive officer in J R's company, with a commission to write two hours of "zebra music" for a wildlife film, and with a foulmouthed teenager named Rhoda for a roommate. Around page 500, the novel reaches a second plateau: Gibbs has the good fortune to win big at the horsetrack and to enjoy a brief affair with Amy—a calm before the storm—and J R is doing well enough to move his operations to the Waldorf with Typhon's former PR man Davidoff "on deck stamping out brush fires" for him. But Eigen has lost both his job and his family, Amy's worst fears soon come to pass when she learns that Lucien has abducted Francis to Geneva, and Norman Angel, faced with the loss of both wife and business, shoots himself with his childhood rifle. The storm breaks loose, and the final third of the novel races at breakneck speed as the J R Corporation spins wildly out of control (ruining a dozen other companies, thousands of careers, even a town or two), Bast succumbs to nervous exhaustion, Indians revolt, a civil war breaks out in Africa, and the stock market collapses.[8]

Asked by an interviewer in 1968 what his work in progress was about, Gaddis answered, "Well . . . ah, just tell them it's about money."[9] Money is the first word in *J R* and it functions as the novel's thematic center of gravity, trapping art, education, commerce, politics, and marriage in its pull. But the novel is more specifically about the difference between "the things worth having" and "the things worth being," as Gaddis wrote in *The Recognitions* (499)—or in *J R*'s financial vocabulary, the difference between tangible and intangible assets. During their final conversation together, an exhausted Bast pleads with J R: "listen all I want you to do take your mind off these nickel deductions these net tangible assets for a minute and listen to a great piece of music, it's a cantata by Bach cantata number twenty-one by Johann Sebastian Bach damn it J R can't you understand what I'm trying to, to show you there's such a thing as as, as intangible assets?" (655). It is this commitment to such intangibles as art, manners, and ideals that sets Bast, Amy, and the artists (in their better moments) apart from the rest of the novel's characters. The contrast is not the trite one between hard-hearted businessmen and tender-hearted artistic types; rather, it is the difference between those who treat others and even themselves as marketable commodities, who measure the validity of any idea by what William James called its "cash-value" (*Pragmatism, passim*), as opposed to those who reiterate Aristotle's "reproach to be always seeking after the useful does not become free and exalted souls" (571), [10] those few people who would not only "rather hear a symphony than eat" (659) but who insist on the human use of human beings. While Bast and Amy intuit this position and try to share it with J R, it is the polymath Jack Gibbs who gives it historical breadth and intellectual fiber.

The Protestant Ethic and the Spirit of Capitalism

When, in his drunken elation at winning the double, Gibbs facetiously invites Amy to join him in redeeming the Protestant ethic (477), he revives a concept Gaddis introduced in *The Recognitions,* probably by way of Max Weber's classic study *The Protestant Ethic and the Spirit of Capitalism* (English trans. 1930). Weber attributes Puritanism's success in capitalist Europe and especially in America to its work ethic, a kind of "worldly asceticism" that held one best serves God by laboring in a "calling," and that the most reliable sign of belonging to the Elect (those predestined for salvation) is financial success in that calling. Its grimmest form was taken by Wyatt's New England ancestors: "Anything pleasurable could be counted upon to be, if not categorically evil, then worse, a waste of time. Sentimental virtues had long been rooted out of their systems. They did not regard the poor as necessarily God's friends. Poor in spirit was quite another thing. Hard work was the expression of gratitude He wanted, and, as things are arranged, money might be expected to accrue as incidental testimonial" (*R* 13–14).

Although its religious nature has been lost sight of today by all but fundamentalists—who remain convinced that wealth is a sign of God's grace—the Protestant ethic continues to exert a baleful influence, of which Jack Gibbs is all too aware. "The Puritan wanted to work in a calling," Weber writes, "we are forced to do so." [11] But the difficulty of finding a calling, of finding something worth doing, is a problem that plagues many of Gaddis's characters. Wyatt raises this complaint in *The Recognitions* (143, 589)—as do Otto and Ed Feasley (620, 615)—but Gibbs locates the problem in a wider historical context: "the whole God damned problem's the decline from status to contract" (393; repeated on 509, 595), that is (to quote from Gibbs's probable source), "from an inherited state of affairs to one voluntarily contracted." [12] In a well-known essay on Tolstoy and Kafka, Philip Rahv sketches the implications of this shift:

Status is synonymous with the state of grace; and he who has a home has status. This home, this cosmic security, this sacred order of status, is not a mythical or psychological but an historical reality. It persisted as a way of life, despite innumerable modifications, until the bourgeois era, when the organization of human life on the basis of status was replaced by its organization on the basis of free contract. The new, revolutionary mode of production sundered the unity of the spiritual and the temporal, converting all things into commodities and all traditional social bonds into voluntarily contracted relations. In this process man was despirited and society atomized; and it is against the background of this vast transformation of the social order that the meaning of the death of Ilyich and K. becomes historically intelligible. [13]

It is against this same background that *J R*'s more perspicacious characters struggle. How many people today can dignify their job as a "calling"? Robbed of the security and sanctification of traditional occupations, most people voluntarily contract themselves to do something hardly worth doing in the first place, much less doing well, leaving only company loyalty (as Hyde insists) in place of social and religious bonds. "No no listen look," Gibbs tells Amy, "first time in history so many opportunities to do so God damned many things not worth doing" (477).

Gaddis's artists face the difficulty not only of finding something worth doing, but succeeding at the task. In their darker moments, Gibbs, Eigen, and Bast wrestle with the same dilemma that drove Schramm to suicide: "It was whether what he was trying to do was worth doing even if he couldn't do it? Whether anything was worth writing even if he couldn't write it?" (621). In an economy still driven by the Protestant ethic, artists labor under the Puritan prejudice against artistic creation—an invalid calling that was considered frivolous at best, at worst sinful and sacrilegious. [14] The attitude toward artists held by Governor Cates, for example, is reminiscent of that attributed by Hawthorne to his Puritan forefathers in the "Custom-House" preface to *The Scarlet Letter:* "A writer of story-books! What kind of business in life,—what mode of glorifying God, or being serviceable to mankind in his day and generation,—may that be? Why, the degenerate fellow might as well have been a fiddler!" Compare this to Davidoff's admission to Bast that he once started to write a novel: "maybe a little jealous of you boys with a knack for the arts luxury I can't afford never finished it, couldn't just sit on my butt and indulge myself like that" (540). Given a society where art is dismissed as a luxury, a knack, an indulgence, is there any wonder that Schramm is driven to suicide and the others to paralyzing self-doubts? If "Blessed is he who has found his work," as Gibbs quips (116, quoting Carlyle), then damned are those who cannot work at the one thing they feel is worth doing—which gives the ubiquitous use of "God damned" by Gibbs and Eigen ominous theological overtones.

Cates, Davidoff, Hyde, and many others in the novel view artists as disruptive neurotics and are convinced that if society could rid itself of these elements it could get on with business (see Cates on 693). Gibbs documents the contributions technology has made towards this goal by helping to eliminate "the offensive human element" (174) from the arts. These range from such unsuccessful ventures as that by "nineteenth-century German anatomist Johannes Müller [who] took a human larynx fitted it up with strings and weights to replace the muscles tried to get a melody by blowing through it [. . .] Thought opera companies could buy dead singers' larynxes fix them up to sing arias save fees that way get the God damned artist out of the arts all at once, long as he's there destroy everything in their God damned path what the arts are all about" (288), to more successful inventions as the player piano ("play by itself get to shoot the pianist" [604]), and in our own age, as Hyde boasts, "Records of any symphony you want reproductions you can get them that are almost perfect, the greatest books ever written you can get them at the drugstore" (48). Cates insists that the book publishing industry is the worst run business in America, but allows, "cut out that ten percent royalty these scoundrels grab they might see a little daylight" (422).

Yet "these scoundrels" alone are capable of redeeming the Protestant ethic, of restoring the human element to a society where "value," "charity," and "good will" exist primarily in their tax law connotations (201, 212, 213), where investment brochures are called "literature," and where "the human machine" (30) is the most prevalent metaphor. Wearily assuring her lawyer that she knows preferred stock doesn't vote, an exasperated Amy goes on:

—Doesn't sing doesn't dance doesn't smoke or drink or run around with women, doesn't even . . .

—Pardon?

—Oh nothing Mister Beaton it's all so, just so absurd so, lifeless, I can't . . .

—Please I, Mrs Joubert I didn't mean to make an emotional issue of it, the . . .

—Well it is! It is an emotional issue it simply is! because there aren't any, there aren't any emotions it's all just reinvested dividends and tax avoidance that's what all of it is, avoidance the way it's always been it always will be there's no earthly reason it should change is there? that it ever could change? (212)

Weber could be used to extend Amy's reductive view to say that's the way it's always been after Puritanism saddled America with "a capitalistic way of life" that "turned with all its force against one thing: the spontaneous enjoyment of life and all it had to offer,"[15] and there's no reason it should change as long as artists remain excluded from America's closed system. Gaddis introduces the second law of thermodynamics early into his novel (21) to remind readers of "nature's statistical tendency to disorder, the tendency for entropy to increase in isolated systems."[16] Recurrent infusions of energy are necessary to combat entropy and homogeneity, and art is the principal means of infusing energy and diversity into a culture's "system." To continue the mechanical metaphor, socially conscious art such as Gaddis's provides invaluable "feedback," which Wiener defines as "a method of controlling a system by reinserting into it the results of its past performance."[17] Gibbs's historical survey *Agapē Agape* and Gaddis's own novel assess the results of America's past performance. "Boy what a mess" (81) is one child's succinct verdict.

Out of the Mouth of Babes

Although Gaddis's most informed social criticism is given to his adult characters, he follows an American tradition in giving his most trenchant criticism to children. If Hawthorne's Pearl is American literature's first underaged critic of Puritan hypocrisy and its socioeconomic ramifications, she leads a children's crusade that includes Mark Twain's Huckleberry Finn, several of James's girls and Anderson's boys, Salinger's precocious kids, and Pynchon's Spartacus Gang. Gaddis modifies and greatly extends the traditional literary use of a child as "the touchstone, the judge of our world—and a reproach to it in his unfallen freshness of insight, his unexpended vigor, his incorruptible naïveté," taking up the tail end of that tradition Leslie Fiedler has so brilliantly analyzed when the innocence of the child is revealed "as a kind of moral idiocy, a dangerous freedom from the restraints of culture and custom, a threat to order."[18] Gibbs lectures his students that "Order is simply a thin, perilous condition we try to impose on the basic reality of chaos" (20), and Gaddis's children are intent on exposing the holes in the various kinds of order adults have tried to impose on society.

Of the many advantages young characters offer, Gaddis is most interested in their blunt honesty, the honesty of a child free enough from "the restraints of culture and custom" to point out the emperor has no clothes. Here, for example, is J R on banking practices: "you know what they do there? Like they say they pay this lousy four and a half percent on savings what those cheap shits never tell you they pay it on your lowest balance the whole quarter so you put like this thousand dollars in for awhile then you take out like nine fifty so you get like a fourth of this lousy four and a half percent of like fifty dollars while they been out loaning this here thousand all the time" (169–70). Those sentiments may be held by Gaddis's adult characters—and by Gaddis himself—but the breezy freedom of J R's language reduces bankers to the level of loansharks and gives his criticism a force it would lack coming from an adult. Rhoda is equally blunt on the kind of business mail J R's "uptown headquarters" receives, especially the "literature" sent out by companies to their stockholders:

—This reduced fully diluted shares outstanding by sixteen percent which had the effect after imputed interest on like you call that literature man I mean I call it bullshit . . . Paper tore, —here's one will you chair this management symposium on healing the sick corporation I mean that must be some chair. [. . .] you could like go chair that thing on healing the sick corporation with your heart batting for the poor they'd really be asthonised man like I never saw such sick companies, I mean that must be some fucking chair. (556–58)

This kind of comic reduction is also used to deflate the pretense of "corporate democracy" by which those same sick companies allegedly operate. Davidoff begins the following discussion, which leads to an argument over the validity of corporate democracy between J R and his classmate Linda:

—that's what people's capitalism is, isn't it everybody. As one of the company's owners you elect your directors in a democratic vote, and they hire men to run the company for you the best way possible. When you vote next spring . . .
—With one share we get like one vote?

—You certainly do, and what's more you're entitled to . . .

—And like if I owned two hundred ninety-three thousand shares then I'd get like two hundred ninety-three thousand votes?

—That's not fair! [Linda objects] Like we get this one lousy vote and he gets like two hun . . .

—What's so not fair! You buy this here one share so you've got like this lousy twenty-two fifty working for you where I've got like six thou, wait a second . . . the pencil came up to scratch, —nought times nought is . . .

—He couldn't could he?

—I could so boy I could even vote two hundred ninety-three thousand times for myself for a director if I wanted to couldn't I?

—I mean like that's democracy? It sounds like a bunch of . . . (92–93)

Linda is cut off before she can give it a name, but J R sees that corporate democracy is actually a plutocracy, and his bullying enthusiasm for it underscores the greed for power at its heart, not to mention its sterility ("nought times nought is . . ."). It is worth noting that Linda and Rhoda join Amy in her condemnation of business practices, to be joined by Liz in *Carpenter's Gothic*; Gaddis's women are usually more humane than his men.

Where Huck Finn spurns the corrupt civilization handed down to him, J R gleefully accepts it, wanting only to know how quickly he can get his share. By following the letter of the law in defiance of its spirit, he is able to engender a "family" of companies with the assistance and example of adults as bereft of humane values as he is. Such respected members of the business community as Cates, Moncrieff, and Crawley are shown to be the moral equivalents to an ambitious sixth-grader by way of dozens of demeaning parallels. J R and Cates share the same attitude toward lawyers ("trouble with you lawyers, all you do is tell me why I can't do something instead of how I can" [196; cf. 336, 467]), react to news of death with financial considerations foremost (J R on 299, 343, Cates on 691, 698, 709), and justify objectionable business deals on the grounds that if they don't do it first someone else will (659, 693); both even examine their snot after blowing their noses (109, 301). J R models his shabby family of companies after Cates's and thus, baffled at Bast's objections to his increasingly outrageous schemes, can legitimately claim he is following in the footsteps of a man Davidoff describes as "one of your country's outstanding Americans[, . . .] one of the men who opened the frontiers of America as we know it today" (91). J R's activities strike him not only as perfectly legal, but even patriotic, as he tells his shyster lawyer: "Look

I'm in a hurry but boy Nonny I mean don't you ever say I told you to do something illegal I mean what do you think I got you for! I mean if I want to do something illegal what do I want with a lawyer I mean holy shit where do you think we are over at Russia? where they don't let you do anything? These laws are these laws why should we want to do something illegal if some law lets us do it anyway" (470).

J R of course has his youth and the moral vacuum in which he lives to excuse his amoral behavior: "holy shit Bast I didn't invent it I mean this is what you do!" (466). The real targets of Gaddis's satire are the politicians, lawyers, businessmen, and educators who invented and sustain "it"—which J R's cynical school superintendent defines as "a system that's set up to promote the meanest possibilities in human nature and make them look good" (463). Even though Gaddis's children unwittingly provide a good deal of the humor in *J R*—Crawley's Mannlicher rifle comes out "manlicker" in the Hyde boy's ordnance-heavy school report (a sly dig at Crawley's hunting machismo?)—they emerge as the real victims of modern society. Several children are shot, killed, or abandoned in the novel; schoolgirls are seduced by their teachers; and technological "enervations" (649) rob them of any chance at getting an adequate education. In this "novel about futures" (a subtitle Gaddis discarded), their outlook for the future is bleakly symbolized near the end of the novel in a newspaper account of "the brave little fourth grader trapped in the soaring steel structure" on a wind-swept Cultural Plaza that does indeed offer "a unique metaphor of man's relation to the universe" (671–72). Weber had warned that the Protestant ethic could become "an iron cage,"[19] but even he did not guess it would imprison children as well. The youngest victim is Eigen's four-year-old son David; asked by his mother if he loves her, he replies in the only terms he understands:

—Yes.
—How much?
—Some money . . . ? (267)

Filthy Lucre

—Money . . . ? in a voice that rustled.
—Paper, yes.
—And we'd never seen it. Paper money.
—We never saw paper money till we came east.

—It looked so strange the first time we saw it. Lifeless.
—You couldn't believe it was worth a thing. (3)

The novel's opening exchange reminds the reader that paper money—along with stocks, bonds, debentures, etc.—is lifeless, inert, having no more intrinsic value than the green leaves the little girl folds into her purse thirty pages later. But Gaddis invests money with a darker hue and important psychological implications by way of a pattern of imagery generated from Freud's symbolic equation of money with excrement. Freud and his followers have traced the route by which a child's anal–erotic satisfaction at producing feces is transferred and increasingly sublimated as he or she grows older: from such substances as mud, sand, tar, putty—all similar to excrement but odorless and socially acceptable—to stones and artificial products such as marbles and buttons, and finally to shiny coins.[20] At this stage, coins appear to the child more valuable than paper money because more reminiscent of feces, as Dan diCephalis learns to his distress when his daughter Nora tells him that her younger brother sold his father's money to some boys: "He didn't know, he thought the coins were better because the other's only paper" (314). By the time a child learns that, contrary to appearances, paper money is more valuable, the transference is complete and the anal–erotic basis of the interest in money is completely sublimated. However, such colloquial phrases as "filthy lucre" and "stinking rich" betray an unconscious memory of money's antecedents, and in *J R* Gaddis does not miss an opportunity to debase financial dealings by alluding to their excremental origins. He knew what he was about when he named the leading businessman-collector of *The Recognitions* Recktall Brown, but in *J R* he approaches Swift in the virulence of his use of scatalogical imagery to reduce commerce to "childish nonsense" (199).

Switching channels from Ann diCephalis's resource program on silk production to Amy's on corporate democracy, Hyde inadvertently introduces the excrement theme in his enthusiasm to give "these youngsters a sense of real values, my boy there . . .

——when the silkworm starts to spin it discharges a colorless . . . that happens in the large bowel before . . . billions of dollars, and the market value of shares in public corporations today has grown to. . . . (46)

This juxtaposition of excrement and money is the first in a series of increasingly blatant metaphoric associations: Hyde's boy dismisses the contents of J R's portfolio as "crap," while J R himself prefers the expletive "holy shit," an oath taken up in moments of stress by Bast and Davidoff (446, 540); J R's first financial deal involves the removal of a pile of dirt in front of Hyde's house—later dignified as "landfill operations" (529), but reminiscent of a child's fondness for mud as a surrogate for excrement; J R picks up a number of tips for starting his business while eavesdropping in Typhon's executive washroom, and once again the Hyde boy can be relied upon to bring out the anal overtones: "go ask that old fart [Cates] that caught us in the toilet you'll find out you don't own shit" (129). Even jokes contribute to the symbolic equation of finance and anality; J R asks Bast, "Did you ever hear that one about if you need money just ask my father he's got piles?" (133), and one of J R's companies makes novelty toilet paper rolls with the message "On the hole business is very good" (581, 681; "The top man in the company he had cases sent out to all the division heads, sort of an encouraging word when you're in the middle of . . ." [682]). Numerous other examples could be piled up, ranging from casual obscenities to Crawley's suggestion that Bast use his aunts' old stock in Norma Mining for toilet paper (173) to J R's plans to have a water tower painted to resemble a roll of toilet paper.

Near the end of the novel, Gaddis brings his excremental vision of the American free enterprise system to an appropriately disgusting climax when, during Isadore Duncan's enema, the two terms in the symbolic equation money = excrement become one:

—No such thing as free enterprise in this country since the Haymarket riots [Duncan says], the minute something threatens this expanding capital forma ow . . .

—That's it lie still now [the nurse tells him], just try to keep it in as long as you can that's it . . .

—Threaten this expanding capital formation and they're at the head of the line whining for loan guarantees against the, the taxes on those tips she's sitting out there counting at night on her four dollar davenport to, to . . .

—That's it now just keep it in . . .

—to bail them out because she's the only one who knows failure's what it's really all, all I don't know how much longer I . . .

—Just a little longer you're doing fine . . .

—See the debt burden rising twice as fast as income the price of chemicals today see that in the paper? Price of chemicals in the human body it's worth three dollars and a half used to be ninety-eight cents when I, I can't, good time to sell out try to slow down inflation the whole security market's co, collapsing credit shrinkage forcing a, can't . . .

—Just a minute longer . . .
—forcing a, a mass, massive outflow of . . .
—Wait here's the pan! here's the pan! my. . . . (684–85)

Excrement is the body's waste, and by this point in the novel commerce should epitomize "what America is all about, waste disposal and all" (27; cf. 25, 179), a veritable wasteland where economic activity amounts to little more than "shitting around" (173) with paper trash.[21]

In this context, Mozart's remark "believing and shitting are two very different things"—quoted in Bast's lecture on Mozart (42) and often repeated by Gibbs—can be read as the bluntest of formulations on the difference between those committed to "intangible assets" and those obsessed with tangible ones. Davidoff names some basic texts of this latter group when he tells J R's biographer "go up to the library dig out some of the President's speeches whole Protestant work ethic head of General Motors on free enterprise whole utilitarian pragmatism angle what works, [J R] sees how things are not how they ought to be whole approach is what works" (530). But he betrays the anal character of the pragmatic approach when he describes his working relationship with his new boss as "he does the grunting and we do the work" (526). In marked contrast stand the believers who, like Gibbs, are "trying to believe something's worth doing long enough to get it done" (492) and are unpragmatic enough to prefer envisioning how things ought to be. The working relationship between members of this group is memorably conveyed in a quotation not from Mozart but from Beethoven: "the better among us bear one another in mind" (290).

If money = excrement, then J R's repeated exclamations of "holy shit" during his financial dealings underscore the extent to which money has become sacred to his sort, the inevitable result of a Puritan ethic that could compare "the relation of a sinner to his God with that of a customer and shopkeeper."[22] Christ had warned them against trying to serve two masters—"Ye cannot serve God and mammon" (Matt. 6:24; cf. *R* 889)—so they ingeniously blended the two together, a figure for whom "holy shit" is a suitable invocation. (An allusion to another famous New Testament text against wealth [Matt. 19:24] is given an anal taint when Duncan tells Bast he's reaching for the bedpan, "Not the eye of a needle" [686].) During their last conversation, Bast rages at J R with all the anger of Christ driving the moneylenders from the temple: "And stop saying holy shit! it's all you, you want to hear holy you're going to hear it" (655) and proceeds to

play him an aria from Bach's twenty-first cantata. Art is holy in the
etymological sense of being whole, characterized by perfection and
transcendence. Bast and the other artists know that such perfection can
only be attempted, never fully realized, but also know, as Johan Thielemans has remarked, that "artistic perfection represents the only possible escape from entropic processes."[23] For them, as for Eliot in "East
Coker," "there is only the trying. The rest is not our business."

To be sure, Gaddis's artists have their faults and in fact bring most
of their misfortunes on themselves. This is not a novel about saintly
artists versus corrupt businessmen. Gibbs displays appalling insensitivity at times, even when sober, and can never seem to remember to
visit his daughter on their court-appointed days; Eigen is an insuffer-
able egotist who turns every conversation his way, and like Gibbs is
often quite sexist. From what we hear of Schramm's and Schepperman's
off-stage actions, they sound self-destructive and more often drunk
than not. Gaddis is as hard on his artists as Melville is on the title
figure of "Bartleby the Scrivener"—another story of Wall Street—and
like Melville illustrates the perils of "preferring not to" engage in conventional behavior. However, the artists are distinguished from the
businessmen in their devotion to ideas loftier than profit margins and
tax shelters. It is with them as with Richard Wagner, of whom Robert
Donington has written: "With a genius—and not only with a genius—
the very thing which goes most wrong with his outer life may often
go most right with his inner life, in the sense that the deeper levels of
his work show an appreciation of the very truths and realities which
most elude him in his personal life-story."[24] Devoted to "the inner
life," artists will naturally be incomprehensible to those committed to
"the outer life." To plunder Eliot again, "Shrieking voices / Scolding,
mocking, or merely chattering, / Always assail them" ("Burnt Norton"), yet by listening instead to the voice inside, Gaddis's artists can
redeem their chaotic lives—and in works of genius, the chaotic lives
that surround them—with something more memorable than a bal-
anced stock portfolio.

The Soft Machine

Duncan's grim joke about selling out, as though his body were a
share in Allied Chemical, recalls the self-alienating consciousness that
Weber and Marx considered inevitable in a capitalist economy. Norman O. Brown summarizes their argument as follows:

The desire for money takes the place of all genuinely human needs. Thus the apparent accumulation of wealth is really the impoverishment of human nature, and its appropriate morality is the renunciation of human nature and desires—asceticism. The effect is to substitute an abstraction, *Homo economicus,* for the concrete totality of human nature, and thus to dehumanize human nature. In this dehumanized human nature man loses contact with his own body, more specifically with his senses, with sensuality and with the pleasure-principle. And this dehumanized human nature produces an inhuman consciousness, whose only currency is abstractions divorced from real life—the industrious, cooly rational, economic, prosaic mind. Capitalism has made us so stupid and one-sided that objects exist for us only if we can possess them or if they have utility.[25]

Amy has already been quoted on the abstract, dehumanized element in commerce, which J R uses to his advantage as he flaunts the "know your broker" rule with characteristic anal imagery:

—like I mean this here bond and stock stuff you don't see anybody you don't know anybody only in the mail and the telephone because that's how they do it nobody has to see anybody you can be this here funny lookingest person that lives in a toilet someplace how do they know, I mean like all those guys at the Stock Exchange where they're selling all this stock to each other? They don't give a shit whose it is they're just selling it back and forth for some voice that told them on the phone why should they give a shit if you're a hundred and fifty all they. . . . (172)

The worst consequence of the "inhuman consciousness" Marx warns against is the tendency to treat people like machines, a tendency the educators in the novel display with frightening insensitivity and that J R displays in abundance with a naïveté that makes it all the more frightening.

The encroachment of mechanization in modern society is viewed with alarm throughout *J R,* especially by Gibbs. In his *Agapē Agape* he derives the mechanization of man not only from such significant but predictable quarters as factories and assembly lines, but from Aristotle's fanciful discussion of robots and automated machinery, E. L. Thorndyke's work in animal intelligence (which, as Gibbs points out, laid the foundations for public school testing), F. W. Taylor's efficiency engineering, and B. F. Skinner's behaviorism.[26] The modern result is the tendency, as Hyde puts it, to

—key the human being to, how did you put it once Dan? Key the . . .
—The individual yes, key the technology to the individ . . .

—Dan knows what I'm talking about, key the individual to the technology. (224)

Hyde's inadvertent transposition of terms is the grounds for Gibbs's complaint "God damned things in the saddle and ride mankind" (400, quoting Emerson). The phrase "in the saddle" is used elsewhere in its sexual slang sense (155, 535), and Coach Vogel, for one, finds a sexual allure in machinery. Regaling Dan with his observations on a school-girl's walk, Vogel comments:

—Look at that rise and fall, just look at that! they came up on the corridor, —look at that reciprocating beam motion and you can see what got Newcomen started on the steam engine can't you. [. . .] Frightening thing how machinery can give you ideas like that about a simple schoolgirl. Start off with that steady reciprocating movement and the next thing you know you've got a bottom, round and droops a little but still good, nothing wrong with it at all. It's when you add that socalled parallel motion James Watt introduced that you've got ass, push pull, push pull, quite an improvement, always sorry I never got a look at Mrs. Watt. (318)

Encouraged by Whiteback to "eliminate the offensive human element" from sexual education, Vogel obliges with a hilarious mechanical model:

—Micro Farad yes that's, farad's an electrical unit, his resistance at a minimum and his field fully excited, laid Millie Amp on the ground potential, raised her frequency and lowered her capacitance, pulled out his high voltage probe and inserted it into her socket connecting them in parallel, and short circuited her shunt [. . .] bar magnet had lost all its field strength, Millie Amp tried self induction and damaged her solenoid [. . .] fully discharged, was unable to excite his generator, so they reversed polarity and blew each other's fuses. . . . (329–30)

These examples suggest that satire can defuse the threat of mechanization, to some extent, simply by ridiculing it. But satire is an adult response largely unavailable to the child, the real victim of technology in *J R*. Dan's daughter Nora likes to pretend her brother is a coin-operated machine (56) and J R sees no substantial difference between "wrecked up buildings and people" (300), and is in fact anxious to replace his employees with machinery simply because "they let you like pretend it's going to wear out two or three times as fast so you're getting this big bunch of tax credits right off, they call it depreciated acceleration or something only the thing is you can't do it with people see" (296). He is lost in admiration for an automat clerk who "throws out twenty nickels without she doesn't even look at them? Like her fingers can count them like they're this here machine" (113) and at school sits through resource films that make extensive use of "the human machine" analogy (30). As a result, it is hardly surprising that he would confuse vivisection with autopsy (77, 129) or believe Eskimos are stuffed for museum exhibits (475). So divorced from real life are J R and his classmates that Gibbs tells Amy, "I could sit down over there shoot myself through the head they'd think I was dead and expect to see me in school tomorrow" (118).

The economist F. H. Knight has written: "Economic relations are *impersonal*. [. . .] It is the market, the exchange opportunity, which is functionally real, not the other human beings; these are not even means to action. The relation is neither one of cooperation nor one of mutual exploitation, but is completely non-moral, non-human."[27] For no one is the market more real than human beings than for Governor Cates, and his nonhuman relation with others is boldly literalized by his own increasing mechanization, in much the same manner as Victoria Wren's in Pynchon's *V.* In and out of the hospital throughout the novel to be fitted out with more prosthetic parts, Cates is finally accused by Zona Selks of "impersonating himself":

—he's nobody, he's a lot of old parts stuck together he doesn't even exist he started losing things eighty years ago he lost a thumbnail on the Albany nightboat and that idiot classmate of his Handler's been dismantling him ever since, started an appendectomy punctured the spleen took it out then came the gall bladder that made it look like appendicitis in the first place now look at him, he's listening through somebody else's inner ears those corneal transplants God knows whose eyes he's looking through, windup toy with a tin heart he'll end up with a dog's brain and some nigger's kidneys why can't I take him to court and have him declared nonexistent, null void nonexistent why can't I Beaton.

—Well it, it would be a novel case ma'am I doubt if there are precedents and the time it would take to adjudi. . . . (708)

Beaton's legalistic response makes him sound as inhuman as his employer, but four pages later he unexpectedly emerges as one of the few victors in *J R* against the dehumanized world it dramatizes. Portrayed throughout the novel as a legalistically precise, rather prissy character ("man he sounds like this real fag," Rhoda reports [554]), the general counsel to Typhon International endures the often humiliating demands made by Cates, Davidoff, and Zona Selk with what may appear to be the spineless loyalty of a company yes man. But Beaton's ardent admiration for Amy—to which he haltingly confesses early in the novel (214)—leads him to plot a devious course of revenge against his tormentors and of triumph for the woman he so admires, a double plot that Gaddis brings to an exciting climax near the end of the novel. Beaton is entrusted by Cates to keep an eye on the date on which the fourth dividend must be declared to retain control of the two foundations in Amy and her son's names; control over both will revert to Amy if the dividend goes undeclared, and throughout the novel Cates reminds Beaton to notify him of the date. Beaton is also aware that one of the products of Nobili Pharmaceuticals contains an ingredient that can be fatal if taken in combination with such strong cheeses as Stilton (207–8); knowing both that the obnoxious Zona Selk is using that product (434) and that she enjoys Stilton cheese, Beaton invites her to Cates's hospital room on the day the fourth dividend must be declared, and even provides her with both drug (690) and cheese (695). All of this comes to a head on page 712, the last day of the novel: as Zona begins gasping for water after taking the drug and cheese, Beaton calmly informs a dumbstruck Cates that he has allowed the fourth dividend to pass, and that Amy's failure to sign over powers of attorney—another delaying tactic of his—means she is now in full control of the foundations and much of Typhon itself. While Cates and Zona suffer what appear to be fatal attacks, Beaton quickly leaves the hospital room for the nearest restroom and promptly throws up from the unbearable tension. There he meets Bast, who has also just thrown up; pale, shaken, and purged, the novel's two unlikely heroes share a moment of quiet solicitude before Bast leaves to make his final trip uptown.

The Human Use of Human Beings

Beaton's heroic (if criminal) course of action needs to be spelled out because it can easily go unnoticed in the blizzard of financial talk that surrounds him. (No reviewer or critic has mentioned it.) Bast's victory is of a different sort: fired from the J R Corporation because of his insistence on what amounts to the human use of human beings (639),

broken in health and spirit, he makes one final attempt at something
worth doing by writing in his hospital bed a piece for unaccompanied
cello "because all they'll give him is a crayon," his roommate Duncan
explains, "he said he has to finish something before he dies" (675). But
he loses all faith in his abilities after the poignant death of Duncan,
who expires wishing only that he had been able to hear Beethoven's
"Für Elise" as it was meant to be played, having heard only the man-
gled version his daughter struggled with before her premature death
at the hands of incompetent doctors (687). Even this crass, garrulous
wallpaper salesman yearns for the perfection and wholeness art can provide, and Bast offers to play the piece for him before he realizes Duncan
is dead. (Another victim, apparently, of medical negligence; all three
of Gaddis's novels are filled with loathing for the medical profession.)

In his fever, Bast had called Duncan his father (671), and there is a
sense that with Duncan's death he is freed from the life-long pressure
he felt from his father to excel at composing. At any rate, he stuffs his
cello music into a wastebasket, in despair over "the damage I've caused
because they all thought what I tried to do was worth doing and I
haven't even done it . . .!" (715). But after his cousin Stella confronts
him with "this fear you haven't inherited James' talent so you'll settle
for money" (716), Bast realizes his failure has resulted not from insuf-
ficient talent but from the misguided use of music to win the love of
his distant father and destructive cousin. Vowing "No, no I've failed
enough at other people's things I've done enough other people's damage
from now on I'm just going to do my own, from now on I'm going to
fail at my own here those papers wait, give me those papers" (718), he
retrieves his cello music from the wastebasket. Beginning where he
should have started originally—with a modest cello piece rather than
an opera—Bast purifies his art by abandoning hopes to win affection
and approval (or fame or fortune) with it. Realizing he not only can
write music but must write it ("genius does what it must talent does
what it can, that the line?" Gibbs had teased him earlier, quoting
Bulwer-Lytton [117]), Bast is last seen, like Wyatt and Thoreau before
him, resolved to live deliberately: "God damn it will you just go do
what you have to and . . . " Eigen tells him, to which Bast responds,
"That's what I'm doing yes!" (725).

"In Gibbs' universe order is least probable, chaos most probable,"
Wiener writes in *The Human Use of Human Beings,* referring not to his
namesake in *J R* but to American physicist Josiah Willard Gibbs. "But
while the universe as a whole, if indeed there is a whole universe, tends

to run down, there are local enclaves whose direction seems opposed to that of the universe at large and in which there is a limited and temporary tendency of organization to increase."[28] Beaton and Bast create such enclaves in their efforts to bring order to the corporate and artistic worlds, respectively, and do so by engaging in what Wyatt in *The Recognitions* called "moral action," which he insists "is the only way we can know ourselves to be real, [. . .] the only way we can know others are real" (*R* 591). Such action ensures the human use, rather than the mechanical use, of human beings. True to Beethoven's dictum "the better among us bear one another in mind," Beaton acts to remove financial control from the morally corrupt and heartless Cates and Zona Selk to place it in Amy's hands. Bast acts morally when he rescues his music from the wastebasket (i.e., rescues art from the wasteland culture that surrounds it), realizing he owes it to himself, not to others, to pursue his music; only by being true to his art can he create art that will be true for others.

The other artists in *J R* are last seen moving in a similar direction. Like Wyatt finding in Esme the necessary lines to complete his portrait of Camilla, the painter Schepperman sees in an old man what he needs to finish a portrait begun long ago. When the old model finally breaks away, his slammed door "brought down half the ceiling," Eigen tells Bast, so now Schepperman is "down on his knees picking plaster out" of the wet paint (724–25). The roof may be falling in on art everywhere, but the artist persists, down on his knees if necessary. Eigen himself has taken up with Schramm's father's attractive young widow and seems intent on working up Schramm's notes into the book Schramm could never write. Eigen represents a more compromised version of the artist enduring, with some unsavory implications: he pretends the notes are actually his, and there's some truth in Rhoda's blunt accusation "you're like some fucking graverobber aren't you" (616)— but the direction he has taken promises to heal two broken marriages, free his writer's block, and, if he can finish the book, vindicate somewhat Schramm's suicide.

Gibbs's case is more vague. Promising Amy he will work on his book during her absence, he accomplishes very little in the 96th Street apartment (a microcosm of the chaotic world an artist must work in), justly complaining that writing a book today is like nursing an invalid back to health (603–5). Convinced like Bast that he is going to die (on the basis of an incomplete blood test), Gibbs too dies to his old life by killing off his alter-ego Grynszpan and begins anew at the end of the novel. Realizing his infatuation with Amy is as misplaced as Bast's for Stella, he tells Amy over the phone (in the disguised voice of an old black retainer) that Gibbs has disappeared. He is last reported reading to Schepperman from Broch's *The Sleepwalkers.* Whether Gibbs will return to *Agapē Agape* or go on to incorporate it into a new, larger work (like *J R?*) is unclear. But told by the doctor he'll live another fifty years, his ex-wife off his back, his romantic idyll with Amy behind him, he too is ready to begin again to live deliberately.

As with Wyatt, the new beginnings for these artists are tentative, not triumphant. As Wiener implies, art is only "a limited and temporary tendency for organization to increase" and will always have to struggle against a universe running down and against people speeding up the process by viewing everything "at the corporate level," as Hyde says. Gaddis's *J R* is a damning vision of what America looks like from the corporate level, and thus a powerful argument for the necessity of recovering the human level.

Chapter Five
J R: Empedocles on Valhalla

The Recognitions draws extensively, even ostentatiously, on world literature and myth to provide structural analogues and colorful parallels to Wyatt's progress and to give historical resonance to his struggles. *J R* uses a comparatively smaller yet equally significant set of literary allusions, deployed more sparingly and more realistically. While the bulk of the allusions in the first novel are to works of personal crises, largely concerning the salvation of the soul, those in the second novel are to works of cultural crises, concerned with the salvation of a society. They fall into three general categories: first and most important is Richard Wagner's operatic tetralogy *The Ring of the Nibelung,* an epic response to the growing mechanistic materialism of the mid–nineteenth century that dramatizes the disastrous results of "loveless egoism and the desire for power and gold."[1] This sense of cultural crisis, shared by Wagner's contemporaries Carlyle, Marx, and Thoreau—to name only those mentioned in *J R*—also animates the works by those in Gaddis's second provenance of literary allusion, a set of Victorian writers consisting of Tennyson, Kipling, Wilde, and Conrad. A third matrix of allusions is drawn from the classical world: Empedocles' cosmology, the darker elements of Greek myth (Typhon, Erebus, Charon, the Erinyes), and Philoctetes, who emerges as the model for Gaddis's artist–hero. These allusions are small voices crying in the wilderness of *J R*'s financial discourse and consequently can easily go unheard during a first reading. But like Gibbs's *Agapē Agape* they provide important cultural and historical underpinnings for the contemporary American crisis depicted in *J R* and fulfill Eliot's prescription for a "historical sense [. . .] not only of the pastness of the past, but of its presence."[2]

While many characters in *The Recognitions* can toss off nearly word-perfect quotations from a variety of texts, the characters in *J R* more realistically mangle or misattribute quotations. Gibbs advises Eigen "read Wiener on communication, more complicated the message more God damned chance for errors" (403). Literary culture is complicated enough that it too is subject to error—errors rarely corrected by anyone in Gaddis's text. On one occasion Eigen does correct Gibbs's misquotation from Hart Crane's "For the Marriage of Faustus and Helen" (621), but it is left to the reader to correct Gibbs's deliberately misleading attribution of the Greek motto over J R's school to Empedocles (45; actually by Marx); his misquotations (usually because drunk) of Yeats, Donne, and others; Amy's opinion that *Carmen* was initially a success (116; it was a failure); and other misattributed quotations that confuse Shakespeare with Marlowe (630) or Mark Twain with Cummings (684). Literary allusions, like everything else in *J R,* are presented in fragmented or elliptical form, shorn from their original contexts; but when threaded together, they display a remarkable thematic coherence and consistency that effectively allow a novel occupied with a few frantic months in the early 1970s to encompass, like Wagner's *Ring,* the beginning and end of the world.

Wagner's *Ring of the Nibelung*

Among the reviewers of *J R,* only Robert Minkoff seems to have noted the presence of *The Ring* in the novel, and among later critics only Steven Weisenburger has devoted any space to this crucial subtext.[3] It would not be going too far to say, as Weisenburger does, that Wagner's *Ring* is to *J R* what the *Odyssey* is to Joyce's *Ulysses.* Although Gaddis's novel, unlike Joyce's, lacks a scene-by-scene, character-by-character correspondence with its model, it alludes to Wagner's work throughout on literal, symbolic, and formal levels. Bast is first introduced rehearsing a chaotic school production of *The Ring* at a Jewish temple(!), with teenaged Rhinemaidens and a Wotan played by a sulky young girl "freely adorned with horns, feathers, and bicycle reflectors" (33). J R has volunteered to take Alberich's part to get out of gym and makes off with the makeshift Rhinegold (the sack of money for his class's stock share) at the end of a scene that comically but effectively sets out *The Ring*'s basic conflict between love and greed.[4] Thereafter, this literal production recedes (like the Rhine at the end of *The Rhinegold*'s first scene) and its teenaged cast is replaced by more symbolic counterparts in the business world where, as Wieland Wagner once remarked, "Valhalla is Wall Street."

Wagner himself was the first to underscore the modern economic implications of *The Ring.* Writing in 1881, five years after the first performance of the complete tetralogy, he argued:

Though much that is ingenious and admirable has been thought, said and written concerning the invention of *money,* and of its value as an all-powerful cultural force, nevertheless the curse to which it has always been subject in song and story should be weighed against its praises. There *gold* appears as the demonic throttler of mankind's innocence; so, too, our greatest poet has the invention of *paper money* take place as a devil's trick. The chilling picture of the spectral ruler of the world might well be completed by the fateful ring of the Nibelung as stock portfolio.[5]

It was George Bernard Shaw who first developed the thesis that Wagner's *Ring* is a critique of predatory capitalism and the morally corrupt status quo. His clever and insightful book *The Perfect Wagnerite*—the source of a memorable aphorism in *The Recognitions* (552) and perhaps the inspiration for Gaddis's adaptation of the opera—argues from Wagner's revolutionary activities and the philosophic nature of the opera itself that Alberich forswears love "as thousands of us forswear it every day" to establish a Plutonic empire that is Wagner's "poetic vision of unregulated industrial capitalism as it was made known in Germany in the middle of the nineteenth century by Engels' *The Condition of the Working Class in England in 1844.*"[6] Opposing the dwarf are the gods— representing church and state—who have as little use for love as Alberich does (Wotan is willing to sacrifice Freia, the goddess of love, to gain his fortress Valhalla) and who have let themselves "get entangled in a network of ordinances which they no longer believe in, and yet have made so sacred by custom and so terrible by punishment, that they cannot themselves escape from them." Wotan relies on Loge, whom Shaw calls "the god of Intellect, Argument, Imagination, Illusion, and Reason," to extricate him from his contract with the simple but honest giants who have built his fortress, and who likewise forswear love and agree to accept gold in lieu of Freia. Sinking deeper into corruption, Wotan and Loge descend to Alberich's Nibelheim to steal the gold Alberich has produced via the ring he fashioned from the Rhinemaidens' gold. By the end of the first opera in the tetralogy, gold and/or its attendant lust for power has corrupted everyone but Loge— who expresses his contempt for the gods in a significant aside—and the Rhinemaidens, whose lament ends *The Rhinegold*: "false and base / [are] all those who dwell above."[7]

Shaw sees in this prelude "the whole tragedy of human history and the whole horror of the dilemmas from which the world is shrinking today," dilemmas rooted in the exploitation by capitalists of a disenfranchised working class, a subjugation supported by the political and religious structures still firmly in place by "the end of the miserable century" when Shaw published the first edition of his book. Shaw's socialist reading of *The Ring* accounts for only one of its many levels, but it is this level that Gaddis uses to reinforce his characterizations and to give a mythic resonance to his novel. The parallels between J R and Governor Cates, for example, take on greater subtlety when they are compared to those between Alberich and Wotan. Wagner's god is a noble, tragic figure who is all too aware that his willingness to compromise his ethics reduces him to Alberich's level of greedy power-mongering and admits as much when he refers to himself in *Siegfried* as "Light-Alberich" to the other's "Black-Alberich." As Deryck Cooke notes, "Wagner made Alberich and Wotan opposite sides of the same coin, representing two complementary images of man-in-pursuit-of-power."[8] Cates shows none of Wotan's self-awareness, but he does develop a grudging respect for J R as he learns more of his financial dealings (433) and unwittingly makes use of Wotan's same light/black imagery with his mistaken assumption that J R's company is run by a "couple of blacks" (431). Nor does Cates show any of Wotan's shame-facedness as he works his financial deals; where Wotan turns away in dejection as he haggles with the giants in order to take possession of Valhalla ("Deep in the breast / burns the disgrace"), Cates displays an amorality as empty as J R's in pursuit of a goal suitably represented by a different kind of Valhalla: "you saw the site of the new parent world headquarters building up the street, you saw the sign? Nothing but a big hole there now" (195) and a hole it remains at the end of the novel as Cates perishes as surely as Wotan does but with none of the renunciation that dignifies the god's self-annihilation.

Where Cates suffers in comparison with his counterpart in *The Ring,* J R wins some sympathy in his role as Alberich. Wagner's dwarf is driven by revenge and malice to become the "sworn plutocrat," as Shaw calls him: after the Rhinemaidens spurned him, Loge explains, "the Rhinegold / he tore in revenge from their rock," and once empowered by the ring he uses it to enslave his fellow dwarfs and to threaten the gods themselves with enslavement. Although J R does cry out "Hark floods! Love I renounce forever!" as directed (36), love renounced him long before: he doesn't seem to have a father, only a mother whose odd hours as a nurse apparently leave him alone more often than not. He is indifferent to girls (like many eleven-year-olds), but he seems to have no friends other than the Hyde boy. Amy is the only one who notices

"There's something a little touching about him, [. . .] he's such an eager little boy but, there's something quite desolate, like a hunger . . . " (246–47) and the reader should share her sympathy for "that bleak little Vansant boy" (497). Where Alberich uses the Tarnhelm to make himself invisible in order to spy on and torment his workers, J R's Tarnhelm is a telephone with a handkerchief stuffed in the mouthpiece, used in a ludicrous attempt to remain "invisible" to his business contacts and associates. It should be noted that J R never buys himself anything in the course of the novel but is lavish in the (unwanted) gifts he bestows on Bast, not to mention well-meant tax advice and a foundation to enable him to continue composing. Alberich hurls curses and imprecations when he loses his empire; J R only sniffles and complains with some justification that he is a boy more sinned against than sinning. And although J R remains amoral and no wiser at the end—except that next time he'll go after banks first—he never becomes immoral, as Alberich does by the end of Wagner's tetralogy.

Amy Joubert's sympathy for J R extends to Bast and Gibbs as well, and she moves between the well-propertied world of Typhon International and their grubbier world of Long Island much as Brünnhilde does between the supernatural and human realms in *The Ring*. "It is Brünnhilde," George G. Windell writes, "the goddess transformed into a human being when her pity for Siegmund led her to disobey Wotan's command, who serves as intermediary between the old, corrupt reign of the gods and the new world, which will be redeemed by human love."[9] Amy is more explicitly associated with Wagner's Valkyrie in the *Dutton Review* version of *J R*'s opening pages: first described as a "high-bosomed brunette," Amy has her counterpart in "a high-bosomed well-biceped Valkyrie bearing aloft a dead warrior on her pommel" in one of the visual aids to Bast's lecture (the final text drops "high-bosomed").[10]

The parallel is inexact—Amy is Cates's grandniece, not his daughter as in the Wotan/Brünnhilde relationship—but Amy exhibits many of the same traits that characterize Wagner's heroine. Brünnhilde receives Alberich's magic ring as a love token from Siegfried and is indifferent to its capacity to wield power. Valuing love over power, she tells her sister Valkyrie Waltraute that she will not return the ring to the Rhinemaidens even to save the gods: "My love shall last while I live, / my ring in life shall not leave me! / Fall first in ruins / Walhall's glorious pride!" (*Twilight of the Gods* 1.3). Amy shows a similar spirit of defiance, first in marrying Lucien Joubert against her parents' wishes, then turning her back on her failed marriage and debutante world to take up "teaching school out in the woods somewhere just to have something to do," she explains to Beaton, "something alive to do even if it's, even if I hardly know what I'm teaching them just following the lesson guide but it's something it's, something" (211). Amy likewise follows Brünnhilde in her willingness to marry beneath her class: "if Daddy could just see the only men I've met I can imagine getting into, into anything with them he'd die, one's probably Freddie's age[11] he drinks and plays the horses his face is like the, he laughs and his face is just torment and, and his hands and the other's a boy, a composer and he's just a boy just all, all radiant desolation and he's dear" (213). Amy alone discerns these qualities (albeit somewhat romanticized) in Gibbs and Bast, as she alone is able to discern J R's better qualities.

Although she has a brief affair with Gibbs, she marries neither him nor Bast but an associate of Typhon named Richard Cutler, a step she had earlier dismissed as absurd: "that would be like, like marrying your issue of six percent preferreds [. . .] avoidance payable semiannually" (214). Amy's loveless marriage to Cutler at the end of the novel has its parallel in Brünnhilde's "marriage" to Gunther, the foolish king of the Gigichungs, made under the mistaken assumption that Siegfried has abandoned her for Gunther's sister Gutrune. Brünnhilde acts to avenge herself against her faithless husband; Amy apparently acts to avenge herself against a faithless family more concerned with its financial interests than the welfare of its children. Realizing that financial power is the only way to regain control over her life and the lives of her retarded brother Freddie and her son Francis, Amy marries the deferential Cutler apparently to be in a better position to wrest financial control out of the hands of the men who have controlled her life for so long. At the end of *The Ring* the Rhinemaidens regain the Rhinegold from the gods, dwarfs, and men who have misused it; at the end of *J R*, male dominion is similarly extinguished as women attain control over most of the assets fought over throughout the novel. Amy, Boody Selk, and Stella Angel are in this regard the Rhinemaidens of the novel, but there is little evidence that they will use their "Rhinegold" more responsibly than their male relations did. None of the three makes the heroic self-sacrifice that redeems Brünnhilde at the end of *Twilight of the Gods,* nor does love play a significant part in their calculations.

By this point it should be obvious that Gaddis is as free in his use of *The Ring* as Wagner was in his use of the Nibelung legends. Gaddis identifies Stella with Freia, for example, but here he leaves Wagner aside and returns to the original Norse myths. Wagner's Freia is weak and (along with her brother Froh) one of the blandest characters in *The Ring,* showing none of the pronounced sexuality of her Norse original. Such characterization is appropriate for *The Ring;* Freia is little more than a cipher, Cooke explains, because she "stands as the goddess of love in a world which has rejected love. [. . .] In the world of *The Rhinegold,* ruled over by Wotan, love does not exist—or rather, it has shrunk into the weak, helpless, hunted figure of Freia."[12] Unlike Gaddis, Wagner makes no mention of Freia's famous necklace Brisingamen, a symbol of her rampant sexuality which a late account in the Icelandic *Flateyarbók* says she won "by sleeping one night in turn with each of the four dwarfs who forged it." To this account, H. R. Ellis Davidson adds in a note: "Students of Freud will recognize the significance of a necklace for a fertility goddess (cf. the ring in Rabelais). It illustrates the familiar tendency to represent the sexual parts of the body by others higher up, and by ornaments worn on these."[13] Students of Gaddis will recognize all of these elements in *J R,* from the bawdy humor regarding Miss Flesch's tendency to rub everybody's face in her *Ring* (26–27, 313), to the necklacelike scar around Stella's neck (from a thyroid operation) that also takes on sexual connotations. But it is Gibbs, Stella's former lover, who makes explicit the identification of Stella with Freia. Learning from Bast that Schramm used to talk to the young composer about "Freya and Brisingamen," Gibbs responds, "Well Christ I could have told you about that Bast I told him about Brisingamen, seen the necklace around her throat I know every God damned link in it have to talk to you about her Bast" (282), but he saves his revelations for Eigen: "Didn't want to tell Bast [. . .] cousin's a God damned witch take you right off at the roots" (407). Like Venus, Freia/Freya is principally associated with sexual love, but she is also one of Graves's dangerous White Goddesses associated with witchcraft and emasculation. Gibbs taunts Stella about this aspect by facetiously offering her the ingenue lead in his hypothetical comedy *Our Dear Departed Member* (74), book by the witch-hunting authors of the *Malleus Maleficarum* (398, 407).

All this learned wit at Stella's expense has its justification in her calculating efforts to gain control of General Roll, largely by captivating then destroying her male rivals with her sexuality. "There were beautiful witches after all," Stella admits (61), but her sexuality is the sterile, destructive opposite of that represented by Wagner's Freia. She apparently married Norman Angel only because he had earned a substantial number of shares in her father's company, but they sleep in separate beds and have had no children. Her sexuality is directed instead at Bast and Gibbs (both of whom she tries to seduce in order to win their shares in the company) and at a mysterious foreign lover who also teases her about Brisingamen (353).[14] Bast welcomes her rather mechanical favors in fulfillment of his long-held desire for her, only to be interrupted by her unsuspecting husband. Bast doesn't realize until the end of the novel that Stella has tried to destroy him and his music in revenge against Bast's mother Nellie, who left Stella's father Thomas for Bast's father James, only to be spurned by the composer James because "he was afraid for anything to come between him and his work" (716). Stella had been blamed by the family for blurting out when much younger the details of the scandal to a neighbor disguised as a gypsy fortune-teller at a fair; her ambition to seize control of General Roll seems motivated less by an urge for power than by a desire to punish the family that has made her so unhappy for so many years. Wagner's Freia is helpless when bartered away by her brother-in-law; Gaddis's Stella means to take Valhalla in return for her mistreatment, and does indeed emerge in control of the company at the end of the book. However, her husband's attempted suicide and subsequent coma seem to have broken her destructive pattern of behavior; Coen tells Bast that her "deeply exaggerated feelings of responsibility" for Norman's attempt "led her to insist on being held by the police" (713), and Stella's recommendation to Vida Duncan to plead for James's return to save the New York Philharmonic suggests she is willing to be reconciled with the family. It is difficult to say for certain; as Coen warns, "her appearance of cold calm I think may be deceptive" (713).

Other characters in *J R* have only superficial resemblances to characters in *The Ring*. Stella's husband Norman, for example, can be associated with the love-sick giant Fasolt, but his interruption of the love tryst between Stella and Edward also links him with Hunding, the hulking husband of Sieglinde, in *The Valkyrie*. Her tryst with her long-lost brother Siegmund has its parallel in that between Stella and her cousin Edward, but even though *The Ring* is alluded to in this scene (142) the principal allusions are to the relationship between the cousins in Tennyson's "Locksley Hall." Similarly, Beaton has a superficial relation to Wagner's Loge, who despises the gods and promises to return the ring to the Rhinemaidens. Beaton likewise plots the downfall of the "gods" of *J R* to return financial control into Amy's hands, but he lacks Loge's wit, irony, and playful intelligence. The Hyde boy sounds like Alberich's brother Mime at one point when he complains "we used to have this neat time trading boy but now everything's . . . " (172), and their schoolmates are consistently called a "horde" as are the Nibelheim dwarfs. Zona Selk sits on Schepperman's paintings much as Fafner the dragon does the Nibelung treasure, but whether Gaddis intended to push the parallels this far is doubtful. Conspicuous in their absence are any clear-cut counterparts to Wagner's heroes Siegmund and Siegfried; Steven Weisenburger makes a tentative case for associating Bast with both on the basis of various incidental parallels, but aside from Siegfried's naïveté, Bast has little of significance in common with either.

Along with putting a number of Wagner's characters into modern dress, *J R* imitates *The Ring*'s uninterrupted formal design. Wagner dispensed with traditional operatic divisions of arias, recitatives, and ensembles in favor of "a continuous, endlessly varied web of melody," as one of Gaddis's sources describes it,[15] built on musical phrases called motifs that identify particular characters, places, objects, and dramatic ideas. Modernist writers such as Mann, Pound, and Joyce make extensive use of literary motifs in their works—a practice parodied by Wyndham Lewis in *The Apes of God*—but Gaddis's *J R* is the most ambitious attempt to do in writing what Wagner did in music (to paraphrase Willie in *The Recognitions* [477]). Length is the first characteristic. *The Rhinegold* alone lasts two and a half hours without a single break; the other three parts of *The Ring* have single acts as long as entire operas by other composers, and use their great lengths to impose their reality on the audience. Bast is especially appreciative of this point; in a discussion of Wagner with Amy, he corrects her assumption that an artist is "asking" an audience to suspend its disbelief: "No not asking them making them, like that E flat chord that opens the Rhinegold goes on and on it goes on for a hundred and thirty-six bars until the idea that everything's happening under water is more real than sitting in a hot plush seat with tight shoes on" (111). *J R* goes on and on for 726 pages of dialogue until the frankly unbelievable story of a sixth-grader's overnight financial success seems more real than the plot of the most plausible novel. While Wagner's lengthy operas are tolerated, however, Gaddis's lengthy novels still meet with resistance, a point worth a brief digression.

In his review of *J R*, George Steiner complains, "All this could have been said compactly, and made accessible to the reader,"[16] a complaint echoed by others who, one suspects, would likewise be satisfied with one of those anthologies that reduces *The Ring's* twenty hours of music to ninety minutes of highlights. Both Wagner and Gaddis attempt a critique of an entire culture, and in Gaddis's case especially the validity of his critique is largely dependent upon his specificity of detail. In this regard, Gaddis resembles Wagner's contemporary Gustave Flaubert, who in his last, unfinished novel attempted to take stock of his culture in much the same manner. Lionel Trilling could be describing Gaddis when he writes of Flaubert in his introduction to *Bouvard and Pécuchet:*

He was unique too in the necessity he felt to see the crisis [the death of culture] in all its specificity of detail. For him the modern barbarism was not merely a large general tendency which could be comprehended by a large general emotion; he was constrained to watch it with a compulsive and obsessive awareness of its painful particularities. He was made rabid—to use his own word—by *this* book, *this* phrase, *this* solecism, *this* grossness of shape or form, *this* debasement of manners, *this* hollow imitation of thought. [. . .] What he wanted to do, he said, was nothing less than to take account of the whole intellectual life of France. "If it were treated briefly, made concise and light, it would be a fantasy—more or less witty, but without weight or plausibility; whereas if I give it detail and development I will seem to be believing my own story, and it can be made into something serious and even frightening." And he believed that it was by an excess of evidence that he would avoid pedantry. [17]

What is lacking in more compact critiques of American manners and mores—Fitzgerald's *The Great Gatsby,* say, or Pynchon's *The Crying of Lot 49*—is the breadth and density of detail that give *J R* its greater weight and plausibility, comprehensiveness and exactitude. Gaddis's novel is as witty as Fitzgerald's and as fantastic as Pynchon's, but easily outdistances either as a critique of the American dream due to the "detail and development" that Gaddis, like Flaubert, pursues with such encyclopedic thoroughness.

Gaddis develops his details in much the same way Wagner develops his musical details in *The Ring.* The entire opera, in one sense, is generated from the opening E flat pedalpoint and the arpeggio figure that represents the Rhine, growing to ninety or so distinct motifs by the fourth part of the tetralogy, by which point nearly every bar contains elements of one or more of these musical ideas. Gaddis imitates Wagner's method by opening with his own pedalpoint, "money," qualified

in the second line as "paper" money (equivalent to the B flat that joins
Wagner's E flat after four bars), which continues to take on further
qualities (Eastern, lifeless, worthless), to become associated with power
(Father), contrasted to silver (i.e., authentic) money, and then impli-
cated in the arts and education—all within fifteen short lines. The
introduction of Julia and Anne's father leads in similar fashion to his
sons, their sibling rivalry, the father's vindictive presence (his ashes
blown back into the sons' beards), and the inevitable entrance of law
to mediate between the brothers and, later, between other conflicting
parties. By the bottom of the first page, then, Gaddis has introduced
all the thematic components of his novel in a way that both imitates
and alludes to *The Rhinegold*. Gaddis's first descriptive sentence—"Sun-
light, pocketed in a cloud, spilled suddenly broken across the floor
through the leaves of the trees outside"—seems to adapt Shaw's description of the "green light" of the Rhinemaidens' underwater play-
ground, where the gold is initially "eclipsed, because the sun is not
striking down through the water."[18] During the first scene of *J R* we
also hear "a tone that seemed to echo the deep" (7)—another allusion
to Wagner's E flat pedalpoint—and the sounds of hammering (10, 16,
etc.), recalling the hammering of the Nibelung dwarfs later in *The
Rhinegold*. At this point Wagner is named for the first time (16), *The
Ring* two pages later, and all of these allusions given a context when
Bast leads his farcical rehearsal of the first scene of *The Rhinegold* later
that day (32–36).

The close parallel with Wagner's opera is dispensed with after this
rehearsal, but Wagner himself is kept in view by dozens of passing
references to his work habits, family life, his other operas, the tuba
that bears his name, even references to Rheingold beer and its Miss
Rheingold competitions in the 1940s and 1950s. One of the companies
J R buys is the Wagner Funeral Homes chain—a witty allusion to
Wotan's Valhalla, a funeral home for dead heroes—whose gay spokes-
person Brisboy is quite entertaining on the problems incurred by such
a name (545). The recurring references to Wagner remind the reader
of the form Gaddis is using, the scope of his enterprise, and the ominous inevitability of the *Götterdämmerung,* which is punningly kept in
the air as Gibbs and Eigen repeatedly "God damn" everything in sight.
(A cellist once told me that musicians pronounce this title "God-damn-
the-*Ring*.")

But most importantly, Wagner is evoked as that rarest of birds, the
successful composer. In his radical lecture on Mozart, Bast cites ex-

ample after example of composers who succumbed to the pressures upon them—"like Franz Schubert dying of typhus at thirty-two yes or, or Robert Schumann being hauled out of a river so they could cart him off to an asylum or the, or Tchaikowski who was afraid his head would fall off if . . . " (43)—indicating that Bast is suffering less from the anxiety of influence than from the anxiety of survival, of whether he too will be destroyed by an indifferent society or be tempted to destroy himself. Noticing Bast's earphone, Brisboy hopes Bast is not going deaf as Beethoven did and pleads with him not to take his life (547); this is a comic misunderstanding at one level, but at another refers to the same pressures that cause Schramm to take his life early in the novel and cause the other artists to wonder, as do Stanley and Wyatt in *The Recognitions,* whether art is worth creating for such an unresponsive, even hostile society. Of all the composers mentioned in *J R,* Wagner alone provides an example of an artist who survived, who created demanding, uncompromising art, and who persisted long enough to see a society that exiled him finally come to him on its knees. Just as Wyatt finally realizes that Titian is a better model than the Van Eycks and their followers, Bast attains something of the iron resolve that drove Wagner to create *The Ring of the Nibelung* against formidable odds, a model that perhaps Bast will someday emulate as triumphantly as Gaddis does in *J R.*

The Victorian Heritage

In the meantime, Bast struggles with setting to music Tennyson's poem "Locksley Hall," one of four nineteenth-century British works alluded to with some frequency in *J R.* Tennyson's poem, Kipling's "Mandalay" and Wilde's "Impressions of America," and Conrad's *Heart of Darkness* are associated in the novel with Bast, Gibbs, and Eigen, respectively, and are used by Gaddis to broaden the historical contexts of his characters' personal problems. The four older works offer Victorian perspectives on the difficulty of fulfilling obligations to a culture not completely believed in, the temptation to forsake those obligations for unfettered freedom, and the tendency to make romantic fictions of women. Although a number of other Victorians are quoted or alluded to in *J R*—Browning, Bulwer-Lytton, Carlyle, Stevenson, Pater— these four warrant closer attention because of the extended use Gaddis makes of their work.

Searching for a text to express his unrequited love for his recently

married cousin Stella, Bast remembers from school Tennyson's "Locksley Hall" (1842), the dramatic monologue of a sensitive young man
who, spurned by his cousin Amy, resolves to "mix with action, lest I
wither by despair." Tennyson's speaker has difficulty, however, maintaining his optimistic vision of his (and England's) glorious future after
his romantic hopes are dashed. Predicting a loveless future for submis-
sive Amy, he predicts England too will have a bleak future: progress,
he suspects, will be at the expense of the individual, and he expresses
grave doubts over the advances promised by science, democracy, imperialism, and women's emancipation. He is tempted to escape to a
tropical paradise where "never floats an European flag" and where he
can avoid progress altogether, but the true Victorian in him wins out
("I the heir of all the ages, in the foremost files of time")[19] and he
decides at last to join his lot with that of the "Mother-Age."

Bast identifies with Tennyson's protagonist as strongly as most ad-
olescents do when they discover a character who embodies their ambitions and frustrations. The parallels here are numerous: both
characters have been spurned by their beloved cousins, both are or-
phans, both have a romantic, idealistic outlook on life incompatible
with practical reality, and both are faced with that perennial Gaddis
quandary:

> What is that which I should turn to, lighting upon days like these?
> Every door is barr'd with gold, and opens but to golden keys.
>
> Every gate is throng'd with suitors, all the markets overflow.
> I have but an angry fancy; what is that which I should do?
>
> (ll. 99–102)

Tennyson's poem is introduced into *J R* at the end of its first frantic
day, when Bast allows Stella to visit the converted barn behind the
Bast house where he composes. In a scene fraught with sexual tension—conveyed partially by Bast's unconscious manipulation of the
cleft of a beer can, into which he stuffs an earlier intruder's condom—
Stella notices his work in progress on the piano, much to Bast's em-
barrassment, but reacts with polite indifference to Bast's broken
confession of her part in inspiring the work (69–71). Stella returns a
few nights later to look for some paperwork and discovers with Bast
that his studio has again been broken in to and ransacked. In what
Stella later calls an effort to rid Bast of his "romantic ideas about him-

self and everything else" (148) she initiates a passionless sexual encounter, only to be interrupted (though not caught) by her husband Norman. Temporarily unhinged at the violation of his private studio and at the frustration of the interrupted tryst, Bast plays wildly from his operatic suite, taking a cue from the thunder outside and mixing with the Tennyson libretto a number of phrases picked up during a frustrating day in Manhattan with J R's class (142). This mélange of lines from "Locksley Hall"—mocking Amy and her oafish husband and calling down the thunder on their mansion—reminds us that Tennyson's speaker is by turns blustering, naive, self-pitying, and spiteful (as is Bast in his worst moments) and that consequently his valid criticisms of the Victorian social order are undercut somewhat by his histrionic posturing. Bast, to his credit, does not indulge in social predictions as Tennyson's protagonist does, but Stella is correct in thinking Bast would do well to abandon those "romantic ideas about himself and everything else." When Gibbs learns of Bast's operatic suite, he too chides him: "Locksley Hall Christ, next thing you'll shock us with a novel call it the Sorrows of Young Werther" (280). (Gibbs goes on to taunt Eigen with another quotation from "Locksley Hall": "ought to get yourself one Tom wed some savage woman let her rear your dusky . . ." [281].)

Aside from modifying his operatic suite to a cantata, little is said of his musical project until the end of the novel—largely because he is too busy writing two hours of film music for Crawley. Hospitalized with double pneumonia and nervous exhaustion—and in a delirium reciting to the nurse "some poetry about some ancient founts" and "some creepy poetry about the dreary moorland" (670–71, from "Locksley Hall," ll. 188 and 40)—Bast comes close to renouncing Tennyson and all art, much as Tennyson's protagonist comes close to renouncing England for the jungle. But both characters recognize these temptations to retreat and to withdraw as no more than the other side of the same coin of romantic delusion, equally foolish and self-defeating. Both adopt instead a more existential willingness to act in the face of uncertainty and possible failure: Tennyson's protagonist accepts "However these things be" and bids a contemptuous farewell to Locksley Hall and all it represents. Similarly, Bast declares, "No, no I've failed at other people's things I've done enough other people's damage from now on I'm going to do my own, from now on I'm going to fail at my own here those papers wait" (718), and retrieves his discarded cello sketches to begin his art anew on a more modest scale and on a more realistic aesthetic foundation.

Old enough to know better, Gibbs likewise gives his beloved the trappings of a romantic heroine from literature and risks compromising his art by making it dependent upon a woman's approval. Having long admired Amy Joubert from afar, he can hardly believe his luck when she welcomes an affair. He calls Eigen from her apartment to tell him of his good fortune, claiming he has "found a cleaner greener maiden in a neater sweeter land" (494), a tongue-twister repeated several times thereafter, though never accurately. The quotation comes from Kipling's once-popular poem "Mandalay" (1890)—coincidentally in the same trochaic octameter as "Locksley Hall"—a ballad filled with nostalgic longing for the Far East and a distaste for England:

> I am sick o' wastin' leather on these gritty pavin'stones,
> An' the blasted Henglish drizzle wakes the fever in my bones;
> Tho' I walks with fifty 'ousemaids outer Chelsea to the Strand,
> An' they talks a lot o' lovin', but wot do they understand?
>
> Beefy face an' grubby 'and—
> Law! wot do they understand?
> I've a neater, sweeter maiden in a cleaner, greener land!
> On the road to Mandalay. . . .
>
> (ll. 35–42)

The same tropical paradise that Tennyson's upper-class protagonist considered but rejected is here extolled by a lower-class Cockney soldier. Both Victorian characters are drawn not only to exotic lovers but to states of lawless freedom; compare Tennyson's "There the passions cramp'd no longer shall have scope and breathing space" with Kipling's "Where there aren't no Ten Commandments an' a man can raise a thirst." That Gibbs would cite Kipling is revelatory both of the nature of his short-termed relationship with Amy and of the impossibility of its success. Amy is not a part of his world, intellectual or social, despite the fact she teaches at the same school as he. Instead, she is as exotic as Kipling's maiden and just as far removed from Gibbs's real needs and social obligations. During their week-long tryst he may as well be in Mandalay, for he quits teaching, sees none of his friends, and forgets to visit his daughter as usual. All of this becomes apparent to him only after she leaves.

When Amy departs for Switzerland she extracts from Gibbs a promise to work on his book, but while looking through his notes he comes across a short story he once began, punningly entitled "How Rose Is Read" and heavy with literary allusion. The short fragment concludes:

Mention her name and you'd see them, or their sharp edges, surface briefly in the young men's eyes dropped quickly elsewhere once they'd learned how many times she'd read Go lovely Rose, in how many different hands, forcing her door with flowers, fleeing it home to books to flee her there. Elena in Turgenev's On the Eve flung down at two am as elsewhere pages feverishly turned to find her serving tea to friends by one gone back to bed to toss alone till dawn came in another part of town where someone else gave up importuning her shade through Gluck's underworld with a twist of the dial to study in his own unsteady hand of the night before beware women who blow on knots and then take all of an hour to find perhaps it was right to dissemble your love, but why did you kick me downstairs? No book heroine as they wanted, this crowd who would not understand how much more human she was, like old Auda after battle and murder, heart yearning [. . .]. (584)

Within two and a half sentences, allusions to Waller, Turgenev, Gluck, the Koran, Isaac Bickerstaffe, and T. E. Lawrence crowd around to rob Rose of any real identity, reducing her to a "book heroine" of the most artificial sort. Gibbs displays a similar tendency to think of the women he meets in literary terms, to "read" into them qualities that tend to reduce them to literary stereotypes. We recall Gibbs comparing Stella to Freya and to a witch out of the *Malleus Maleficarum*; he associates Amy with Kipling's maiden but first with the woman in Eliot's "Hysteria" (117, 120, 130); after meeting Rhoda he compares her to a variety of figures ranging from a sorceress by Hans Baldung to "Bess, the landlord's daughter" from Alfred Noyes's "The Highwayman" (388). (Eigen picks up Gibbs's allusion to "Mandalay" and gives Rhoda the "beefy face and grubby hand" of Kipling's Chelsea housemaids [615].) At one point Gibbs even resorts to a printing metaphor to describe a woman: "Ann, she's sort of you [Amy] in a cheap edition, twentieth printing of the paperback when things begin to smear" (245).

On one hand, such remarks are just a playful habit on Gibbs's part, the learned banter of a well read man. But on the other hand, they betray a tendency to find excuses, justifications, and ideals in literary works for his own behavior, a tendency more excusable in someone of Bast's age and temperament. Throwing his Tennyson back in Bast's face, Stella refuses to take part in "this whole absurd, her bosom shaken by a sudden storm of sighs this whole frightened romantic nightmare you'd put me into" (716); substitute Kipling for Tennyson and Amy

would find Gibbs doing much the same thing were she not so preoc-
cupied with her own problems. A confrontation like that between Bast
and Stella is unnecessary; Gibbs soon sees that he has been acting like
a Cockney soldier pining away in useless regret and avoids Amy upon
her return. Like her namesake in "Locksley Hall," Amy decides to play
it safe and marry dull Dick Cutler—a nice dovetailing of allusions—
but by that point Gibbs has shaken off his escapist fantasy and thus is
able to avoid the romantic agony that bedevils Bast.

The other Victorian Gibbs most often quotes is Oscar Wilde, whose
bantering lecture "Impressions of America" (1883) figures prominently
in Gibbs's *Agapē Agape.* The lecture is based on Wilde's 1882 tour of
America, where he promulgated doctrines that, as Richard Ellmann
has noted, "constituted the most determined and sustained attack on
materialistic vulgarity that America had seen." More important,
"Wilde presented a theory not only of art but of being, not only a
distinguished personality but an antithesis to getting on without regard for the quality of life."[20] This same annoyance at "getting on
without regard for the quality of life" underlies Gibbs's concerns, and
he shares Wilde's conviction that America is antagonistic toward art.
Noting that "America is the noisiest country that ever existed," Wilde
warns, "All art depends upon exquisite and delicate sensibility, and
such constant turmoil must ultimately be destructive of the musical
faculty" (289). *J R* is the noisiest novel that ever existed, and the efforts
of its artists to create amid its continual turmoil painfully illustrate
Wilde's observation. Gibbs takes as his epigraph to *Agapē Agape* the
notice Wilde saw posted above a saloon-hall piano in Leadville: "Please
do not shoot the pianist. He is doing his best" (288). Wilde playfully
calls this "the only rational method of art criticism I have ever come
across," but Gibbs knows he lives in a shoot-the-pianist culture that
destroys its artists, for in the arts "one's best is never good enough"
(604), as Wilde himself would learn when his country destroyed him.
While Kipling informs Gibbs's romantic urges, Wilde justifies his cultural and artistic fears.

As Bast has Tennyson and Gibbs has Kipling and Wilde, Eigen has
Joseph Conrad. Gaddis makes the same ironic use of *Heart of Darkness*
as Conrad makes of the *Aeneid* and the *Inferno,* putting as much ironic
distance between Eigen and Marlow as Conrad does between Marlow
and Aeneas or Dante. Although there are only two clusters of allusions
to Conrad's 1899 novella in *J R,* they help to illuminate both Eigen's
motives through the second half of the novel and his complicated relationship to his own Kurtz, the suicide Schramm.

The first set of allusions follows Gibbs's and Eigen's meeting with the lawyer Beamish, who has come to see them about settling Schramm's estate. Recovering the copy of the *Malleus Maleficarum* he had once loaned him, Gibbs discovers that Schramm kept a photograph of his young stepmother in its pages. Eigen is immediately taken by the photograph for reasons Gibbs coarsely points out:

—Real number Tom, really see how she made the old man's mickey stand for him can't you Beamish . . .
—Well she, she was a good many years his junior yes, even younger than your friend Mister Schramm himself but . . .
—See why Schramm felt like Hippolytus turned backwards can't you, get a hand on that raw lung see how Schramm felt can't you. (392)

Beamish goes on to say he has some papers for her to sign and Eigen volunteers to take the picture and papers to her. Though drunk, Gibbs is able to point out the obvious parallel a little later that evening when he comes across a copy of *Heart of Darkness* at Eigen's apartment and badgers him about it: "Heart of Darkness, God damned cheerful reading Heart of Darkness, part at the end he takes her picture and letters back to her[, . . .] part she says you were his friend, part she says you knew what great plans he had something must remain wants his last word to live with, part you knock on the mahogany door take the papers up to Mrs Schramm wants his last words to live with believing and shitting are two very different things Mrs Schramm always remember that part" (408).

But just as Marlow delays a year before returning her picture and letters to Kurtz's Intended, Eigen forgets about the papers until he finds them in his pocket a few weeks later. This time a sober Gibbs more bluntly confronts Eigen with his carnal motive for seeing Mrs. Schramm:

—Meet her yes, probably be God damned grateful, shame you can't take [Schramm's] folder along too show her he was on the threshold of great things, might have kicked the world to pieces . . .
—I don't know what you're, why you can't give me this either can you any credit for, credit for any loyalty to his memory my God see him in that canvas sack it's like being loyal to a nightmare . . .
—Had your choice of nightmares go ahead you've got custody of his memory Christ, all you've done for it certainly got the right to sweep it up with the trash why not take that picture he had of her too, see you waiting there in the lofty drawing room her pale face floating toward you in the dusk takes

both your hands in hers no chick but good Christ she's survived hasn't she, probably tell you she knew him better than you did want to hear his last words give her something to live with, dream the nightmare right through to the God damned end when you come out with it . . .

—What with, what do you mean I . . .

—Mean you'd better fix your trousers in front there first that's all. (631)

All the allusions in *J R* to *Heart of Darkness* are to its final third, in which Marlow struggles first to comprehend what Kurtz represents to him, and then with the dilemma whether he should preserve or destroy the Intended's naive illusions about Kurtz. Eigen faces only the former struggle; the latter is inconsequential, for though Mrs. Schramm makes only one brief appearance in the novel (508–9), it is clear that she's little more than an opportunistic young woman who only married the older Schramm for his money. She probably has no illusions about anything, and certainly lacks the Intended's "mature capacity for fidelity." Abandoned by his wife and tormented by sexual frustration, Eigen takes up with Mrs. Schramm (now a wealthy young widow) with basely pragmatic motives that burlesque Marlow's more reverent approach to Kurtz's fiancée. Marlow's dilemma—which, as Gibbs points out by way of Mozart, amounts to choosing between "believing and shitting"—is one Eigen is spared.

Eigen's relationship to Schramm is more problematic. Like Kurtz (with whom he shares a monosyllabic German surname), Schramm left his native land to go abroad, not for Africa and ivory but for Europe to fight in World War II, and there underwent experiences that turned him against his country with as much contempt as Kurtz has for his Belgian company. "The only time he was ever really alive was the war," Gibbs tells Amy, "he was a tank commander in the Ardennes and when it was all over he just never could quite, he has some bad periods that's all" (246). But after his suicide Gibbs reveals that Schramm was taken prisoner by the Germans while trying to defend a small town after the rest of his division had retreated without telling him (390–91).[21] Schramm's efforts to write a book about his experiences fail—partially because of paternal disapproval—though he does manage a screenplay for a western called *Dirty Tricks* that allegorizes the events. But Eigen takes as proprietary an interest in Schramm's notes for this book as Marlow does in Kurtz's papers. Although both Eigen and Schramm are writers, there is no professional rivalry: Eigen has written an important if neglected novel that surely overshadows Schramm's western. He has had difficulty following up that first novel, however, and apparently sees in Schramm's notes the means by which he can overcome his own writer's block and, perhaps, expiate the guilt Gibbs has instilled in him for indirectly contributing to Schramm's suicide. The scuffle for Schramm's notes is as ludicrous as that for Kurtz's papers: Gibbs comes across them in Schramm's typewriter case and reads them, but lies to Eigen that he hasn't seen them (595, 597); when Eigen arrives at the 96th Street apartment to look for them himself, he tells Rhoda the notes are "some work I started" (613); Rhoda, Schramm's last girl-friend and crude enough to compare to Kurtz's savage concubine, tells Eigen he is lying (616), but he finally finds them stuffed under some boxes and is last seen bearing them to Mrs. Schramm's with motives that are mixed, at best.

Gibbs and Eigen, like Marlow before them, bear witness to the com-promises, self-deceptions, and outright lying that paradoxically are sometimes necessary to maintain a realm of ideals, that beautiful world Marlow feels Kurtz's Intended epitomizes so well. She represents the moral imagination which, even if more of a curse than a blessing, is what separates her, Kurtz, and Marlow from the pilgrims, flabby dev-ils, and the other moral bankrupts in Conrad's novella. It is this same moral imagination that, with all their faults, distinguishes Eigen, Bast, Gibbs, and the better characters in *J R* from the rest, and Gad-dis's sparse but incisive use of *Heart of Darkness* underscores the precar-ious artificiality of this moral realm. The four works by Tennyson, Kipling, Wilde, and Conrad share this concern for the validity of cul-tural and moral ideals and the difficulty involved in pursuing them in the face of personal unhappiness and widespread corruption.[22] Gaddis's dramatic update of these concerns and difficulties reminds the reader that culture is always in a state of crisis, and will always demand the most from that minority still convinced culture is worth preserving.

The Classical Heritage

The reference to Hippolytus in Gibbs's discussion of Schramm's fam-ily is one of many allusions to Greek myth and philosophy scattered throughout *J R*. Some of them, like this particular one to Phaedra's love for her stepson, are casual and local in the sense they do not form a particular pattern other than evoking the darker corners of Greek myth. Thus we hear Amy compare the sound of buzzsaws to the Eri-nyes (75) and have companies named after the hundredheaded monster Typhon, the Delphic priestess Pythia, and Erebus, the personification of darkness (and the name of a ship mentioned at the beginning of *Heart of Darkness*). Brisboy wanted to name his funeral home chain after Charon, but his mother "found that a trifle recherché" (545). Plato is mentioned a few times, Heracleitus quoted once, and Gibbs cites Aristotle's *Politics* often in his *Agapē Agape,* but the most important references are to the Greek philosopher Empedocles and to Philoctetes, the wounded archer who ended the Trojan War. The relative paucity of references to these two figures is in inverse proportion to their importance in *J R.*

Empedocles is known to students of literature chiefly as the despairing suicide of Matthew Arnold's poetic drama "Empedocles on Etna," but Gaddis's references are to the original poet–philosopher of the fifth century B.C. and to the extant fragments of his cosmological poem *On Nature.* Empedocles posited a cosmic cycle in which two contrasting forces alternate in control over the world—Love (or amity, harmony, unity) and Strife (or hatred, disorder, division)—and believed that organic life evolves in four stages. The first generation of life consists of disunited limbs: "Here sprang up many faces without necks, arms wandered without shoulders, unattached, and eyes strayed alone, in need of foreheads" (fragment 57). In the second generation, body parts join randomly with others, creating monsters:

solitary limbs wandered about seeking for union [. . .] But as one divine element mingled further with another, these things fell together as each chanced to meet other, and many other things besides these were constantly resulting. [. . .] with rolling gait and countless hands [. . .] Many creatures were born with faces and breasts on both sides, man-faced ox-progeny, while others again sprang forth as ox-headed offspring of man, creatures compounded partly of male, partly of the nature of female, and fitted with shadowy [*or* sterile] parts. (fragments 58–61)

The third generation produces "whole-natured forms," androgynous beings of the sort described by Aristophanes in Plato's *Symposium,* and in the fourth and final generation these beings are sexually differentiated into the human race.[23]

Asked about the pseudo-Greek inscription over J R's school—actually by Marx,[24] a parting joke of Schepperman's—Gibbs refers the writer Gall to "Empedocles [. . .] I think it's a fragment from the second generation of his cosmogony, maybe even the first" (45) and proceeds to paraphrase the relevant fragments, much to Hyde's annoyance:

—I'm trying to have a serious discussion with these Foundation people on closed-circuit broadcast and you butt in with arms and legs flying around somebody's eyes looking for their forehead what was all that supposed to be!

—He was asking about one of the preSocratics, Major, the rule of love and the rule of strife in the cosmic cycle of Emp . . .

—They didn't come here to talk about comic cycles [. . .] (48)

The world according to Gaddis is ruled by Strife, a parodic or "comic" cycle in which fragmentation and division are rampant. In crowded Penn Station where "elbows found ribs and shoulders backs," Gibbs mumbles, "—place is like the dawn of the world here, this way . . . countless hands and unattached eyes, faces looking in different directions" (161). Although here as elsewhere Gaddis literalizes Empedocles' image of random body parts (cf. 406–7), it pervades *J R* more in the metaphoric sense Emerson uses in "The American Scholar": "The state of society is one in which the members have suffered amputation from the trunk, and strut about so many walking monsters,—a good finger, a neck, a stomach, an elbow, but never a man." Emerson is complaining not only of specialization but of fragmentation, of allowing oneself to diminish from Man to a thing, a function, and then treating others likewise. The result is the incomplete creatures who stumble through *J R* bumping into people, using them, misunderstanding others and being misunderstood in turn, each insisting on his or her narrow outlook, and coming together only in strife-ridden marriages, chaotic school systems, or monstrous combinations such as the J R Family of Companies that rival anything in Empedocles. Love, except in the person of Amy (amity), is conspicuous in its absence.

Gaddis creates lexical equivalents to Empedocles' limbs and monsters with his elliptical, fragmented dialogue and a heterogeneous discourse made up of incongruent diction, specialized jargon, mixed metaphors, and tortuous syntax. Examples are unnecessary; open any page of *J R*. What protects the novel from the charge of merely recreating the lexical chaos it deplores, however, is the selective ordering of the artist, where *this* particular idiotic comment is chosen from many others and placed next to *that* one, so that together they echo a remark made in a dissimilar context elsewhere, and in turn anticipate a line from Tennyson, and so on. *J R* does indeed look chaotic, but it is a "perfectly ordered chaos" (*R* 18) created to fight Strife with strife with the strongest bow Gaddis can wield.

Philoctetes, Gaddis once explained to an interviewer, "was the hero with the bow, the great champion of the Greeks, who goes into the sacred garden where he's not supposed to be and is bitten by the snake, and has a festering wound and they get rid of him, they exile him. Then, when there's trouble and they need him and his bow, Ulysses and the prince [Achilles' son Neoptolemus] come and say, 'Please, come and help us.' And that idea has always fascinated me."[25] In *J R,* Philoctetes is most closely associated with James Bast, the composer of an opera called *Philoctetes,* and living abroad in self-imposed exile. He is called back at the end of the novel to save the ailing New York Philharmonic in much the same spirit as Philoctetes is called back to end the Trojan War. But in a larger sense, Philoctetes is the prototype of all of Gaddis's troubled and troublesome artists; his limp is shared by both Schramm and Gibbs, and the latter especially manages to save a number of companies by the novel's end despite (or perhaps because of) the "festering wound" of his bitter sarcasm. In *The Recognitions,* Basil Valentine offers Wyatt the epigram "the priest is the guardian of mysteries. The artist is driven to expose them" (261). The artist is accursed for profaning the sacred garden, and yet the insight and power gained from the transgression is sorely needed by the very society that curses him when those mysteries are used for fraud and oppression. Among artists in general, the satirist especially is driven to expose mysteries, an act that opens him to charges of disrespect, impiety, pessimism—further terms can be culled from Gaddis's harsher reviews—and yet the health of any society is dependent upon the satirist's corrective lash, as Pope argues so eloquently in his satires and epistles.

Sophocles makes it clear in his *Philoctetes*—which seems to be the basis for James Bast's version (117)—that the wounded archer has himself to blame as much as anyone for his troubles. Gaddis's artists are no better, frequently given to disruptive, self-destructive behavior, drunkenness, vanity, and callous selfishness. Pope's satirist is a good citizen, but Gaddis's artists are closer to Edmund Wilson's conception of Philoctetes and the satirist as hero:

I should interpret the fable as follows. The victim of a malodorous disease which renders him abhorrent to society and periodically degrades him and makes him helpless is also the master of a superhuman art which everybody has to respect and which the normal man finds he needs. [. . .] It is in the nature of things—of this world where the divine and the human fuse—that they cannot have the irresistible weapon without its loathsome owner, who upsets the process of normal life by his curses and his cries, and who in any case refuses to work for men who have exiled him from their fellowship.[26]

This is the nature of the tension that exists between the artists and the businessmen in *J R* and was the subject of the concluding pages of the section on the Protestant ethic in chapter 4. But Gaddis's interest in this theme is obviously personal as well as professional. His first novel ignored by the literary establishment, he must have felt like Philoctetes in exile while staring out the windows of Pfizer International in the late fifties and early sixties, trying to write speeches on balance of payments problems and the hazards of direct investment overseas while other, lesser talents were being lauded. In 1962–63 he had the same commission from the Ford Foundation for a book on the uses of television in the schools that his character Gall has in *J R*, and a more fitting name for this alter ego cannot be imagined. (It also recalls the fact that Philoctetes' arrows were dipped in the gall of the hydra.) Later in the sixties, Gaddis was tempted to take part in protesting against the Vietnam War but realized that his work in progress would make a more permanent statement about the values that led America into the war, so he continued to work in isolation like Philoctetes on the isle of Lemnos. By the time *J R* was finally published in 1975, he had been absent from the literary scene twice as long as Philoctetes had been absent from Troy, but the novel's National Book Award and his subsequent honors, grants, and critical accolades form an ironic parallel to the despised Greek hero's career that Gaddis must have relished. Philoctetes' powerful bow brought an end to the Trojan War; Gaddis's powerful *J R*—the greatest satirical novel in American literature—brings an end to the American dream of "success and like free enterprise and all" (726). Twilight has fallen upon the gods, and the romance of America darkens to Gothic.

Chapter Six

Carpenter's Gothic; or, The Ambiguities

In the years following the publication of *J R,* Gaddis occasionally taught at Bard College, an experience he described as follows:

My friend William Burroughs used to say that he didn't teach creative writing, he taught creative reading. That was my idea in the Bard courses I taught, especially "The Theme of Failure in American Literature," where we read everything from Dale Carnegie's *How to Win Friends and Influence People* to William James' *Pragmatism* to *Diary of a Mad Housewife.* What I was trying to do was raise questions for which there are no distinct answers. The problems remain with us because there are no absolutes.[1]

Carpenter's Gothic is likewise a course in creative reading, a novel that raises questions for which there are no distinct answers, and one that counters absolutes with ambiguities. "There's a very fine line between the truth and what really happens" is a dictum that echoes throughout the novel,[2] but while half the characters proclaim the truth and the other half expose what really happens, an ambiguity that neither half wishes to acknowledge prevents the reader from attaining an absolute certainty about many of the novel's events and returns him or her to the air of uncertainty that is the chief climate of our ambiguous times.

This much can be deduced: *Carpenter's Gothic* concerns the last month in the life of Elizabeth Booth, "a stunning redhaired former debutante from the exclusive Grosse Point area in Michigan" and "the daughter of late mineral tycoon F R Vorakers" (255). Former head of Vorakers Consolidated Reserve (VCR) in southeast Africa, her father committed suicide eight or nine years before the novel opens when his bribery practices were in danger of being exposed. At his funeral, Paul Booth, a Vietnam veteran and proud Southerner (actually an orphan of uncertain heritage) who "carried the bag" for the briberies, seduced Liz (as he calls her) and took her as his second wife. He quickly ran through much of her money in a number of ill-considered schemes to get rich; the rest of her money is tied up in a trust administered by "Adolph," much to Paul's frustration. Four years before the novel's present Liz survived an airplane crash, and four years later Paul is still pursuing a bogus suit for the loss of his wife's "marital services." Financial difficulties have led the couple to quit New York City for a rented house up the Hudson River—a ninety-year-old house in "Carpenter Gothic" style—whence Paul hopes to make it big as a media consultant. As the novel begins, his most promising client is the Reverend Elton Ude, an evangelical preacher from the rural South who with Paul's help parlays an accidental drowning during a baptism into a providential call for a multimedia crusade against the forces of evil, a.k.a. the powers of darkness (namely communism, teachers of evolution, the "Jew liberal press," and secular humanists everywhere). Using the house simply as a place "to eat and sleep and fuck and answer the telephone" (244), Paul spends most of his time elsewhere. Liz's younger brother Billy pays an occasional disruptive visit, but she spends most of her time fighting off boredom and coping with an unending series of phone calls, many concerning the whereabouts of the house's absentee landlord. Enter mysterious stranger.

A man apparently in his late fifties, McCandless began as a geologist and in fact did the original exploration of the African ore field that is now up for grabs between VCR and the Reverend Ude, who has a mission and radio station there. Disgusted at the increasing CIA involvement with the various movements toward independence in Africa beginning in the 1950s, McCandless drifted for years: he married and fathered a son named Jack (who once attended school with Billy), supported himself by teaching and writing articles for encyclopedias and science magazines, and even wrote a novel about his African experiences with the CIA. The first marriage ending in divorce, McCandless married a younger woman named Irene, but she left him two years before the novel opens. He is presently being hounded by both the IRS and the CIA, the latter in the uncouth person of Lester, a former colleague of his African days who is convinced McCandless retains vital information regarding the ore field under dispute.

McCandless arrives one misty morning to reclaim some papers stored in a locked room. Coming to life at his appearance, Liz transforms McCandless into a wearily romantic "older man" with a mysterious past, and on his second appearance a week later takes him into her bed during one of Paul's many absences. McCandless leaves the next afternoon in the company of Liz's brother Billy, whose conversations with McCandless (there and later that night in New York City) solidify his earlier resolve to go to work for his father's company in Africa. Shortly after their departure, Paul arrives home in tatters (the victim of an attempted mugging) with all his media plans in tatters as well. Paul is $10,000 richer—keeping for himself a bribe Ude intended for Senator Teakell and the FCC—and has paid a black youth $100 to assassinate the minister. That night paid arsonists mistake another house for McCandless's and burn it to the ground.

A week later McCandless returns to find the house ransacked and Liz griefstricken at the news of her brother's death aboard an airplane shot down off the coast of Africa, a strike targetted for Senator Teakell who was ostensibly on a fact-finding mission "defending the mineral resources of the free world" but actually watching out for his own financial investments there. McCandless is preparing to leave the country—he has accepted Lester's offer of $16,000 for his papers—but fails to persuade Liz to go with him. After he leaves Liz receives a brief visit from McCandless's first wife, both mistaking each other for the second wife Irene. Alone in the house after she leaves, Liz suffers a heart attack, symptoms of which were displayed throughout the novel, though dismissed by her doctors as high blood pressure. Because the house is still in disarray after the break-in that morning, the press mistakenly reports her death as the result of attempting to interrupt a robbery in progress. Paul believes this story, and though distraught at her death, he loses no time making sure both her and Billy's money will come to him, and he is last seen on the way to their funeral using the same seductive line on her best friend Edie that he used on Liz many years before.

As is the case with any summary of a Gaddis novel, this one not only fails to do justice to the novel's complex tapestry of events but also subverts the manner in which these events are conveyed. Opening *Carpenter's Gothic* is like opening the lid of a jigsaw puzzle: all the pieces seem to be there, but it is up to the reader to fit those pieces together. Paul's refrain "fit the pieces together you see how all the God damn pieces fit together" (205) doubles as Gaddis's instructions to the reader. The author doesn't make it easy: the initials VCR are used throughout the book but not spelled out until thirty-three pages before the end; a letter from Thailand arrives on page 48 but its contents not revealed until two pages from the end; names occur in conversations that are not explained until pages later, if ever. Ambiguity is introduced in the very first line of the novel ("The bird, a pigeon was it? or a dove"),

and though this particular ambiguity is cleared up at the end of the
first chapter ("It was a dove"), the novel is rife with other ambiguities
that are never resolved. Even after multiple readings, several events
remain ambiguous, sometimes because too little information is given,
sometimes because there are two conflicting accounts and no way to
confirm either. As Paul complains later, "pieces fit together problem's
just too God damn many pieces" (212).

Such narrative strategies are designed not to baffle or frustrate the
reader but to dramatize the novel's central philosophic conflict, that
between revealed truth versus acquired knowledge. Nothing is "revealed" by a godlike omniscient narrator in this novel; the reader learns
"what really happens" only through study, attention, and the applica-
tion of intelligence. The reader learns that McCandless has married
twice, for example, by noting that Mrs. McCandless is old enough to
have a twenty-five-year old son (251), but Irene young enough to still
use Tampax (150; cf. the handwriting on p. 31) and to have her youth-
ful photograph praised by Lester (132). If several events remain ambiguous after such study, the reader must live with those ambiguities
rather than insist on absolute certainty, much as the intellectually mature individual abandons the absolutes of revealed religion for the ambiguities of actual life. In this novel Gaddis plays not God but the
philosopher who announced the death of God: "Objections, non-
sequiturs, cheerful distrust, joyous mockery—all are signs of health,"
Nietzsche insists. "Everything absolute belongs in the realm of
pathology."

To his credit, Jesus never spoke of absolutes, but his followers in
Carpenter's Gothic do. The Reverend Ude insists that Christ "builded
this great edifice of refuge for the weak, for the weary, for the seekers
after his absolute truth in their days of adversity and persecution" (80).
The same zealous certainty inspires the efforts of "a charming Texas
couple who keep an eye out for schoolbooks that undermine patriotism,
free enterprise, religion, parental authority, nothing official of course
[McCandless explains to Billy], just your good American vigilante
spirit hunting down, where is it, books that erode absolute values by
asking questions to which they offer no firm answers" (184).[3] The cat-
alog of conservative values here is important: *Carpenter's Gothic* is not
simply a satire on fundamentalism but a critique of the ways such
absolutist thinking can lead to imperialism, xenophobia, rapacious
capitalism, and the kind of paranoid cold war ideology enshrined in a
New York Post headline at the novel's (and perhaps the world's) end:
"PREZ: TIME TO DRAW LINE AGAINST EVIL EMPIRE" (259).

But none of this is new, as McCandless reminds both Billy and Lester in his harangues against Christianity. Just as Marlow in Conrad's *Heart of Darkness* prefaces his tale of European imperialism in Africa with a reminder of Roman excursions into ancient Britain, McCandless several times sketches bloody moments in the history of Christianity (128, 142, 190–91, 236, 243) and locates this militant impulse in the Bible itself: the god of the Old Testament "is a man of war" (243; Ex. 15:3) and the son of god in the New Testament warns his followers "I come not to send peace but a sword" (142; Matt. 10:34). The fundamentalist fervor that McCandless lashes out against is not a topical subject that will date Gaddis's novel, but rather the latest and potentially the most lethal manifestation of a religion that has caused more bloodshed than harmony in its two-thousand-year history. The carpenter of "the profit Isaiah" (80) and the carpenter's son of the gospels together have created a Gothic nightmare of blood, guilt, persecution, righteousness, and intolerance—one meaning of Gaddis's ambiguous title.

"A patchwork of conceits, borrowings, deceptions"

A more important meaning of the title comes late in the book. At an awkward moment in his last conversation with Liz, McCandless welcomes the opportunity to discuss a neutral subject—the house's "Carpenter Gothic" architecture:

—Oh the house yes, the house. It was built that way yes, it was built to be seen from the outside it was, that was the style, he came on, abruptly rescued from uncertainty, raised to the surface —yes, they had style books, these country architects and the carpenters it was all derivitive wasn't it, those grand Victorian mansions with their rooms and rooms and towering heights and cupolas and the marvelous intricate ironwork. That whole inspiration of medieval Gothic but these poor fellows didn't have it, the stonework and the wrought iron. All they had were the simple dependable old materials, and the wood and their hammers and saws and their own clumsy ingenuity bringing those grandiose visions the masters had left behind down to a human scale with their own little inventions, [. . .] a patchwork of conceits, borrowings, deceptions, the inside's a hodgepodge of good intentions like one last ridiculous effort at something worth doing even on this small a scale [. . .]. (227–28)

If one discounts the self-deprecating tone—Gaddis is no "country architect" with only "clumsy ingenuity"—this can easily double as a description of *Carpenter's Gothic* itself. Gaddis found his "simple dependable old materials" in what he described to one interviewer as the "staples" of traditional fiction and set himself a task: "That is, the staples of the marriage, which is on the rocks, the obligatory adultery, the locked room, the mysterious stranger, the older man and the younger woman, to try to take these and make them work."[4] In addition to these staples of plot, he depends on the staples of certain generic conventions. Gaddis's "patchwork of conceits, borrowings, deceptions" brings under one roof a number of genres: the Gothic novel, the apocalypse, the romance (in all senses), and the metafictional meditation, along with elements of Greek tragedy, Dickensian social satire, the colonial novel, the political thriller, documentary realism, the contemporary Vietnam veteran's story, and what Roy R. Male calls "cloistral" fiction. Each is a room jammed into Gaddis's Gothic construction, a little invention (only in comparison to his first two novels) of great ingenuity.

As McCandless says, Carpenter Gothic houses were meant to be seen from the outside and hence were designed with an emphasis on outward symmetry, even if it resulted in such deceptions as "twinned windows so close up there they must open from one room but in fact looked out from the near ends of two neither of them really furnished, an empty bookcase and sagging daybed in one and in the other a gutted chaise longue voluted in French pretension trailing gold velvet in the dust undisturbed on the floor since she'd stood there, maybe three or four times since she'd lived in the house" (226–27). (Note how perfectly this captures Paul and Liz's relationship: united under one roof, they are nonetheless divided by a wall of differences, his intellectual bankruptcy and lust caught by the empty bookcase and sagging daybed, her monied background and pretense to culture exposed by the chaise longue, "neither of them really furnished" with culture, taste, or education.) The novel conforms to strict Aristotelian unities: the action occurs in a single setting over a short period of time, which internal references date October–November 1983.[5] A near-perfect symmetry balances the novel's seven chapters: the first takes place at sunset, the last at sunrise; the second and sixth begin with Liz climbing the hill from the river; the end of the third is linked to the beginning of the fifth with verbal repetitions (cf. 94–95 with 151); the central chapter, the fourth, takes place on Halloween and features the long conversation between McCandless and Lester that provides most of the historical background to the present-day events in the rest of the novel—the central heating of Gaddis's Gothic, as it were.

The Gothic novel is of course the most obvious genre Gaddis exploits in *Carpenter's Gothic,* adapting as many of its stage properties as is feasible: the isolated "mansion," the locked room, the endangered "maiden," the mysterious stranger, even the witching time of year that allows for references to Halloween ghosts and a haunted house (148). The "unwavering leer" of the Masai warrior on a magazine cover follows Paul around as spookily as the moving eyes of an old portrait, and Liz has a dream premonition of death during the unholy hours between All Saints' Eve and the Day of the Dead. A parody of older Gothic novels, *Carpenter's Gothic* also incorporates long quotations from *Jane Eyre,* Charlotte Brontë's parody of even older Gothic novels.

The Gothic mode is not a new departure for Gaddis. Those chapters of *The Recognitions* set in New England creak with Gothic machinery: the heretical priest poring over curious volumes of forgotten lore, the deranged servant, supernatural statues, apparitions, the gloomy atmosphere that hangs over the desolate landscape, and the same attraction/repulsion felt by earlier Gothicists for Italianate Catholicism. Nor is the Gothic mode a new departure for American literature; Leslie Fiedler's *Love and Death in the American Novel* goes to great length to demonstrate that Gothic is the most characteristic form of classic American fiction. At the fleeting disappearance of James's and Wharton's ghosts, the genre took two directions in modern American literature: the Southern Gothic of Faulkner, O'Connor, and early Capote; and the supermarket Gothic that Alexander Theroux has wittily described (in his great Gothic romance *Darconville's Cat*) as "the genre of course of Hoodoo, Hackwork, and Hyperesthesia, the popular dustjacket for which always showed a crumbling old mansion-by-moonlight and a frightened beauty in gossamer standing before it, tresses down, never knowing which way to turn."[6] The New England Gothic tradition of Hawthorne and Melville has had few followers among serious contemporary novelists aside from Djuna Barnes, early Hawkes, some Pynchon, and the occasional anomaly (like Kerouac's *Dr. Sax* or Brautigan's *Hawkline Monster*).

Why would Gaddis revive this outmoded genre in the technological eighties? Partly for the challenge of reclaiming an exhausted genre (as Barth and Sorrentino like to do in general, and as Joyce Carol Oates has done with the Gothic in particular), but largely because the "symbols and meanings" of Gothic, Fiedler points out, "depend on an awareness of the spiritual isolation of the individual in a society where all communal systems of value have collapsed or have been turned into meaningless clichés."[7] Liz's physical and McCandless's intellectual isolation underscore the extent to which both have lost that connection between themselves and the world that McCandless reads of in V. S. Naipaul's novel (150, quoted at the end of chapter 1). With all of Jane Eyre's restlessness but none of her independence, Liz is the persecuted maiden in a Gothic melodrama: "when you feel like a nail everything looks like a hammer," she confesses to McCandless (223), reversing one of his cracks about fundamentalists. Psychologically immured in her Carpenter Gothic tower, Liz's choice between Paul and McCandless amounts to "being the prisoner of someone else's hopes [. . . or] being the prisoner of someone else's despair" (244). Liz finally perishes in that prison, subverting the happy ending of most Gothic fiction.

McCandless has much in common with the Gothic hero–villain, a mixture of Faust, Don Juan, and the Wandering Jew—all coming to stand, Fiedler argues, "for the lonely individual (the writer himself!) challenging the mores of bourgeois society, making patent to all men the ill-kept secret that the codes by which they live are archaic survivals without point or power."[8] McCandless feels Christianity is just such an archaic survival, but his attempts to expose its ill-kept secrets of militarism, misogyny, and superstition have met with failure: called upon to testify at a "creationist" trial in Smackover—similar to one held in Arkansas in December 1981—he learned that fundamentalists are not simply ignorant (lacking knowledge) but stupid (hostile to knowledge), heirs to the anti-intellectual tradition in America that Richard Hofstadter has written about. An intellectual hero of sorts, McCandless is also the villain of the piece, however. He hopes to put his house in order (226), like Eliot's speaker at the end of *The Waste Land,* but he succeeds only in spreading disorder and chaos. Not only is he indirectly responsible for Billy's death, but he is as responsible as anyone for the nuclear showdown that looms over the novel's final pages. Possessing the facts about the ore field, he withholds this information, partly because he won't be believed (239), partly because of the Gothic villain's willingness to see his corrupt civilization go up in flames. During her longest and most powerful speech, Liz hurls exactly this accusation at him:

—And it's why you've done nothing . . . She put down the glass, —to see them all go up like that smoke in the furnace all the stupid, ignorant, blown up in the clouds and there's nobody there, there's no rapture no anything just to see them wiped away for good it's really you, isn't it. That you're the one who wants Apocalypse, Armageddon all the sun going out and the sea turned to blood you can't wait no, you're the one who can't wait! The brimstone and fire and your Rift like the day it really happened because they, because you despise their, not their stupidity no, their hopes because you haven't any, because you haven't any left. (243–44)

The references to apocalypse and Armageddon here toward the end of the novel indicate the Gothic overlaps with another genre, the apocalypse. While the Gothic developed out of Jacobean drama, apocalypse originates in religious writings and mythography, bearing witness to the strange fact that cosmic catastrophe has been a fear and a hope of almost every society—a fear of extinction no matter how richly deserved, and a hope for purgation and another chance to start anew. The literary apocalypse is used by a writer to render judgment on society, a heretical desire to destroy that which God created. God said let there be light; the apocalyptic writer, like Melville at the end of *The Confidence-Man,* puts out the light.

Unlike other modern literatures, American literature has a strong, almost obsessive tradition in apocalyptics. The first "best-seller" in our literature was Michael Wigglesworth's long poem *The Day of Doom* (1662), and since then most of our major novelists have dealt in the apocalyptic: Hawthorne, Melville, Mark Twain, Faulkner, West, O'Connor, and among contemporary novelists, Ellison, Barth, Baldwin, Burroughs, Pynchon, Vonnegut, Coover, Elkin, and DeLillo. It is tempting to divide these into the two traditional camps of apocalypsists—the hopeful and the despairing—but many of these writers display both tempers: *Moby-Dick* is hopeful (Ishmael survives the catastrophe), but *The Confidence-Man* is despairing (nothing follows this masquerade).

Like Melville, Gaddis has written both forms: with Stanley composing a *dies irae* (322) and Willie speaking of "the doctrine of last things" (478), *The Recognitions* is certainly an apocalypse, but because Wyatt survives the cultural collapse that destroys the rest of the novel's characters, it can be called a hopeful one—hence Gaddis's disavowal of apocalyptic intentions in the interview quoted near the end of chapter 1. In *Carpenter's Gothic,* however, both forms of apocalypse are set against each other: Ude and his followers are obviously banking on a hopeful apocalypse when they will be able to enjoy a "space age picnic in the clouds" while the rest of us are frantically consulting our Survival Handbook (135), and consequently they interpret all signs of cultural breakdown in terms of those foretold in the Book of Revelation.

McCandless interprets those same signs in the despairing apocalyptic temper of the Melville of *The Confidence-Man* or the Twain of *The Mysterious Stranger*. And yet, McCandless is himself a mysterious stranger with a nihilistic vision as despairing as Twain's devil's. A Christian reading of *Carpenter's Gothic* would expose McCandless as the antichrist of the novel, spreading despair and disorder everywhere he goes. (The Christian reader might even find correspondences between the novel's seven chapters and the seven seals in Revelation.) While signs and the interpretive context we place them in are themes in the novel, these particular ones are among the "deceptions" of the Carpenter Gothic style, however, and should not be seriously entertained.

Both McCandless and Ude can be held partially responsible for the literal apocalypse that begins at the end of the novel—"**10 K 'DEMO' BOMB OFF AFRICA COAST War News, Pics Page 2**" (259)— but McCandless's sin is only one of omission; Ude's is the more fatal one of commission. Like Tod Hackett in Nathanael West's *The Day of the Locust* (with which *Carpenter's Gothic* has tonal similarities), Gaddis presents fundamentalists' "fury with respect, appreciating its awful, anarchic power, and aware that they had it in them to destroy civilization."[9] Although fundamentalists themselves may seem incapable of doing much more than breaking schoolbus windows and bombing abortion clinics, they are associated throughout the novel with rightwing politicians whose paranoid style of politics (as Hofstadter named it) can indeed help fundamentalists satisfy their apocalyptic yearnings. Fundamentalism or paranoid politics is not unique to America; as McCandless tells Billy:

—The greatest source of anger is fear, the greatest source of hatred is anger and the greatest source of all of it is this mindless revealed religion anywhere you look, Sikhs killing Hindus, Hindus killing Moslems, Druse killing Marionites, Jews killing Arabs, Arabs killing Christians and Christians killing each other maybe that's the one hope we've got. You take the self hatred generated by original sin turn it around on your neighbors and maybe you've got enough sects slaughtering each other from Londonderry to Chandigarh to wipe out the whole damned thing, [. . .]. (185–86)

What the world and the novel need now to counteract this hatred and the polemical tone is love, or at least a romantic subplot. But the possibilities for love in both spheres are limited.

Gaddis's working title for *Carpenter's Gothic* was "That Time of Year:

A Romance," and like the "Gothic" in the published title, "romance" here means many things. As a genre, it has much in common with the Gothic; in fact, the latter is largely the romance pushed to extremes. The romance does, however, place greater emphasis on the picturesque, the idyllic, and the more conventional forms of love. (Love in the Gothic tends toward lust or perversion.) Gothic and romance "claim a certain latitude" from such constraints of realistic fiction as verisimilitude and plausibility, as Hawthorne argues in his famous preface to *The House of the Seven Gables*—another novel centering on a Gothic house and a debilitating family heritage—and Gaddis has always claimed this latitude.

Carpenter's Gothic displays the romance's indifference to strict realism: as in *J R,* events move impossibly fast; its countless coincidences strain belief; and there is an overwhelming emphasis on the negative that would be out of place in a more realistic novel. When Paul opens a newspaper "without knocking over the bottle" (203), the narrator draws our attention to this rare event, because elsewhere, no one can reach for anything without upsetting whatever glass is closest at hand; no one can cook anything without burning it; no one can turn on the radio without hearing a distressing item of news; checks are delayed while bills arrive swiftly; cars and trucks are always breaking down, buses caught in traffic jams; clocks, newspapers, even dictionary definitions are unreliable; the novel is tyrannized by Murphy's Law, where anything that can go wrong does so, and usually at the worst possible moment. Hawthorne insists that the romancer "may so manage his atmospheric medium as to bring out or mellow the light and deepen and enrich the shadows of the picture," and Gaddis has pursued the latter option with such a vengeance that *Carpenter's Gothic* joins Selby's *Last Exit to Brooklyn* and Sorrentino's *The Sky Changes* as one of the darkest novels in contemporary American literature. Even its humor is black.

Only the brief affair between McCandless and Liz admits any light into the novel. Here Gaddis turns from the Hawthornian romance to sport with the Harlequin romance, using every cliché in the style book: the bored debutante–housewife, the older man with an exotic background, the obligatory adultery, the revivification of said debutante after one night in the older man's arms, prompting her to sigh with a straight face, "It's an amazing thing to be alive, isn't it . . . " (151). There is even the offer to take her away to faraway lands and the dutiful decision to stand by her man for reasons she cannot quite articulate;

echoing Stella in Williams's *A Streetcar Named Desire,* Liz can only say, "It's just, I don't know. Something happens . . . " (89).

Gaddis redeems these clichés by subjecting them to much more rigorous artistic control than is common, carefully integrating them with the patterns of imagery and literary allusion at work throughout the novel. Each genre Gaddis adapts has a reference point in a classic text: the Gothic in *Jane Eyre,* the apocalypse in the Book of Revelation (the most frequently cited biblical text), and the romance in the Shakespearean sonnet that provided Gaddis's earlier title:

> That time of year thou mayst in me behold
> When yellow leaves, or none, or few, do hang
> Upon those boughs which shake against the cold,
> Bare ruined choirs, where late the sweet birds sang.
> In me thou see'st the twilight of such day
> As after sunset fadeth in the west;
> Which by and by black night doth take away,
> Death's second self, that seals up all in rest.
> In me thou see'st the glowing of such fire,
> That on the ashes of his youth doth lie,
> As the deathbed whereon it must expire,
> Consumed with that which it was nourished by.
> This thou perceiv'st, which makes thy love more strong,
> To love that well which thou must leave ere long.

When Liz echoes the sonnet's concluding couplet by telling McCandless at the end of the novel, "I think I loved you when I knew I'd never see you again" (245), she unconsciously completes a series of references to the sonnet that begins on the novel's first page. In fact, much in the novel is encapsulated in the sonnet: the autumnal and predominantly nocturnal settings, the recurring references to empty boughs and yellow leaves outside and the fire grate inside—cold until McCandless arrives to rekindle it—and of course the relationship between the older man and his younger lover. Similarly, the poem generates much of the novel's imagery. On those rare occasions when Gaddis's characters stop talking, the text gives way to luxurious descriptions of the dying landscape, passages as colorful as the vegetation they describe, and imitative in their gnarled syntax of the intertwined vines, branches, and fallen leaves.

The equation of autumn with late middle age in the poem's first quatrain is spelled out with scientific precision by McCandless (who had quoted a few words from the sonnet on p. 167):

—all those glorious colours the leaves turn when the chlorophyll breaks down in the fall, when the proteins that are tied to the chlorophyll molecules break down into their amino acids that go down into the stems and the roots. That may be what happens to people when they get old too, these proteins breaking down faster than they can be replaced and then, yes well and then of course, since proteins are the essential elements in all living cells the whole system begins to disinteg. . . . (228–29)

A page later, McCandless picks up the sunset image in the second quatrain of the poem:

—Finally realize you can't leave things better than you found them the best you can do is try not to leave them any worse but they [the young] won't forgive you, get toward the end of the day like the sun going down in Key West if you've ever seen that? They're all down there for the sunset, watching it drop like a bucket of blood and clapping and cheering the instant it disappears, cheer you out the door and damned glad to see the last of you.
But the sun she looked up for was already gone, not a trace in the lustreless sky and the unfinished day gone with it, leaving only a chill that trembled the length of her. (230–31)

In this brilliant orchestration of images, Gaddis combines the literal setting of this conversation and the metaphors from sonnet seventy-three with an echo from Revelation, which Liz will pick up later in the same conversation ("Apocalypse, Armageddon all the sun going out and the sea turned to blood" [244; cf. 185]—all leading to a symbolic alignment of organic decay (leaves, light, people) with cultural decay, and suggesting that fundamentalism is a malign but not unnatural cancer in the body politic, accelerating an otherwise inevitable process. As Cynthia Ozick was the first to point out, "It isn't 'theme' Mr. Gaddis deals in (his themes are plain) so much as a theory of organism and disease. In 'Carpenter's Gothic' the world is a poisonous organism, humankind dying of itself."[10] McCandless "doesn't much like getting old," his first wife will later say (250), nor does he much like watching the disintegration of civilization, but apart from raging against the dying of the light, there's little he can do to halt either.
As Shakespeare's sonnet is a seduction poem of sorts, the words "death" and "expire" probably carry their secondary Elizabethan mean-

ing of orgasm. If so, the trope has its counterpart in *Carpenter's Gothic,*
where a description of Liz after lovemaking (163) is used again to describe her position at death (253). Her death, of course, upsets the
parallel with the sonnet—as it does with the Gothic—but it does fulfill
the expectations of the dove imagery likewise present from the novel's
first page. Watching the neighborhood boys bat a dead dove back and
forth, "a kind of battered shuttlecock moulting in a flurry at each
blow" (1), Liz turns away, catching breath for the first time. Throughout the novel Liz is closely associated with doves and is clearly a kind
of battered shuttlecock herself—literally in her relationship with Paul
(9, 22), figuratively with Billy and McCandless. Once again braving
the dangers of cliché, Gaddis invests Liz with all the symbolic qualities
of a dove (peace, innocence, gentleness) and even has her bleat like a
dove (163–64). The symbolism is self-explanatory, but again Gaddis
manages to make the cliché work: when this "sweet bird" emits "a
choked bleat" as she dies, even a reader hardened by the savage ironies
of modern literature must feel that peace and innocence have indeed
fled from this world for good. The dove of the Holy Ghost is treated
no better by the novel's militant Christians, and at the symbolic age
of thirty-three Liz even has aspects of Him the fundamentalists profess
to worship.

Most of the other genres that have rooms in Gaddis's house of fiction
can be treated more briefly. In its use of a single stage setting and
small cast, its reliance on messengers (by letter and phone), and its
adherence to Aristotelian unities, *Carpenter's Gothic* has the formal design of Greek drama, a subject McCandless once taught (252). Like an
adaptation by O'Neill or Eliot, Gaddis's novel includes a dark heritage
of paternal guilt, features continual offstage atrocities, and even has its
Furies in the neighborhood kids always smirking through Liz's windows. Reviewer Frederick Busch instead found several parallels to
Dickens's *Bleak House,* and rightly so.[11] Gaddis's social crusader in-
stincts encourage the parallel, as does his use of Dickensian names for
his unsavory manipulators (Sneddiger, Grimes, Stumpp, Cruikshank,
Grissom, Lopots). In particular, Gaddis shares Dickens's faith in the
novel as an instrument for social improvement and his ability to make
family disputes representative of larger social disputes. Gaddis goes so
far as to correct von Clausewitz on this point: "it's not that war is
politics carried on by other means it's the family carried on by other
means" (241). The African episodes reported at secondhand are reminiscent of those novels featuring Anglo–Americans abroad that run

from Conrad's *Heart of Darkness* and several books by Forster and Waugh through contemporary novels by Graham Greene, Anthony Burgess, and Paul Theroux—not to mention the multinational political thrillers of more commercial novelists. *Carpenter's Gothic* is also a textbook example of "cloistral" fiction, a genre centering on a mysterious stranger's visit to a closed community and the moral havoc that results, epitomized by such stories as Melville's "Bartleby the Scrivener" and Mark Twain's "The Man That Corrupted Hadleyburg."[12]

Of more interest is Gaddis's contribution to the growing body of Vietnam War fiction. Paul's Vietnam experiences are referred to only sporadically in the novel, but by piecing together the clues his tour of duty can be reconstructed—though only after separating the "official" truth from what really happened. He somehow managed to win a commission as a second lieutenant, much to the contempt of his adopted father, who reportedly told him "that he was God damn lucky he was going in as an officer because he wasn't good enough to be an enlisted man" (91). A platoon leader in the 25th Infantry, Lightning Division, he quickly alienated himself from his men by insisting on "All this military bullshit with these spades from Cleveland and Detroit in his broken down platoon out there kicking their ass to show them what the southern white officer class is all about" (193). After turning in his crew chief, a black nineteen-year-old named Chigger, for using heroin, Chigger "fragged" him; that is, he rolled a grenade under Paul's bed in the Bachelor Officer Quarters. He was pulled out by Chick, his radiotelephone operator, and the Army covered up the incident by blaming an enemy infiltrator—the story Paul later uses. Paul is discharged at the same grade he entered, an indication of his incompetence, for as McCandless points out elsewhere, officers welcome a war for "the chance to move up a few grades, peace time army they'll sit there for twenty years without making colonel but combat brings that first star so close they can taste it" (238). Paul leaves behind a native mistress, pregnant with his child: "it was a boy" he learns at the end of the novel (260).

Paul parlayed his bogus reputation as "this big wounded hero" into a job with Vorakers Consolidated Reserve, but years later, as the novel opens, he is still plagued by terrible memories of Vietnam: the machinegun fire (8), nearly crashing in a helicopter (83–84), and the aftermath of the fragging incident: "you know how long I laid there? How many weeks I laid there blown right up the gut watching that bottle of plasma run down tubes stuck in me anyplace they could get one in? Couldn't move my legs I didn't know if I had any, God damn medic breaks the needle right off in my arm taped down so it can't move can't reach down, dare reach down and and see if my balls are blown off, my balls Liz! I was twenty two!" (45). When a black nineteen-year-old mugger attacks Paul late in the novel, he sees in the mugger's eyes the same hatred he saw in Chigger's and kills him, for "They never taught us how to fight, they only taught us how to kill" (241).

The difficulty Vietnam veterans have had readjusting to society has already become a literary staple, and Gaddis's vets (Chick and Pearly Gates as well) have as difficult a time as any. But Gaddis once again subverts the cliché by portraying Paul as responsible for his own troubles. Not only did he bring the fragging upon himself, but in a sense he joins the enemy—not the Viet Cong, but Vorakers, Adolph, Grimes, and the other power brokers: "God damn it Billy listen! *These are the same sons of bitches that sent me to Vietnam!*" (242). Yet so strong is his lust for prestige and money that Paul willingly sacrifices his sense of moral outrage to join the very power structure that nearly killed him, thereby sacrificing any sympathy his Vietnam ordeal might otherwise have earned him.

The generic text Gaddis uses here as a reference point, though unacknowledged, is Michael Herr's brilliant *Dispatches* (1977), an impressionistic account of the two years (1967–68) Herr covered the Vietnam war for *Esquire,* and an aesthetic exercise in rescuing "clean" information from official disinformation and the vagaries of memory. Gaddis borrows one anecdote from Herr's book ("never happen sir" [214])[13] and perhaps found a number of his other Vietnamese details there: Tu Do street, Drucker's bag of ears, the raunchy language Paul uses on the phone with Chick, and some of the war jargon (sapper, ville, "the old man," greased, BOQ). More importantly, *Dispatches,* like Gaddis's novel, investigates the gap between the "truth" and what really happens, specifically, the Pentagon's pathological allegiance to an official truth that had no basis in reality. The references to Vietnam in *Carpenter's Gothic* act as a grim reminder that his theme is no abstract problem in epistemology but one that in this case left 130,000 American casualties dead, maimed, and missing.[14]

Finally, it should be noted that another writer Gaddis borrows from in *Carpenter's Gothic* is the author of *The Recognitions* and *J R.* Richard Poirier once described Pynchon's second novel, *The Crying of Lot 49,* as "more accessible only because very much shorter than the first [*V.*], and like some particularly dazzling section left over from it."[15] At first glance, the shorter and more accessible *Carpenter's Gothic* might similarly look like a particularly dazzling section left over from *J R*; in fact, one reviewer went so far as to say "its main plot comes from pages 96–103 of *J R*; substitute Liz Vorakers Booth for Amy Cates Joubert, change the African locale from Gandia to somewhere near South Africa, and there it is. Even the names Ude and Teakell come from *J R*."[16] There are important tonal differences between Gaddis's three novels, of course, but it is possible to hear other echoes from the earlier two: Liz may have actually read *The Recognitions,* for she refers to the passage where Arnie Munk got so drunk he folded up his clothes and put them into the refrigerator (13; *R* 175) and to Rev. Gwyon's remark about "the unswerving punctuality of chance" (223; *R* 9), which also appears on Jack Gibbs's page of quotations (*J R* 486). For his third novel Gaddis returned to some of his source books for the first: to the 14th edition of the *Encyclopaedia Britannica* for the Battle of Crécy (147), the *Pilgrim Hymnal* for two militaristic hymns (142), Cruden's *Concordance* for biblical citations, and Eliot's *Four Quartets* for at least one line ("to recover what had been lost and found and lost again and again" [155], from "East Coker"). Even McCandless's novel has its echoes from *The Recognitions,* especially in his protagonist Frank Kinkead's decision "to live deliberately" (139), the same Thoreauvian vow Stephen makes (*R* 900). From *J R* he borrowed Pythian Mining in addition to the other names enumerated above and hints broadly at a connection between J R and Paul Booth when Adolph dismisses the latter as knowing "as much about finance as some snot nosed sixth grader" (209).

Much of this is little more than the kind of cross-referencing one finds in the novels of Faulkner, Barth, or Sorrentino. *Carpenter's Gothic*'s relationship to its huge predecessors seems to be hinted at in Mc-Candless's description of his own novel: "it's just an afterthought why are you so damned put out by it," he asks Lester. "This novel's just a footnote, a postscript" (139). That "this" can refer to both novels, and the fact this particular line occurs in a real novel about an imaginary novel by an imaginary character who resembles a real author calls attention to the ambiguous status of fiction, blurring that fine line between truth and what really happens by offering fine lines that seem all the more true because they never happened. The ontology of all fictions—literary, religious, patriotic, and personal—emerges as one of Gaddis's principal preoccupations in *Carpenter's Gothic* and makes this novel not merely a footnote, a postscript to his megafictions, but a virtuosic exercise in metafiction.

That's All She Wrote

The nature and production of fictions is a recurring topic in the dialogues that make up the bulk of *Carpenter's Gothic,* ranging from Paul's rather primitive notion of literary fiction (112) to McCandless's more sophisticated attacks on such "fictions" as religion, occult beliefs, and ethnocentrism. Gaddis's use of fiction to explore the status of fiction is characteristic of metafiction, that genre that calls attention to itself as fiction and flaunts the artificiality of art.[17] Though more realistic than such exemplary metafictions as O'Brien's *At Swim-Two-Birds* or Sorrentino's *Mulligan Stew, Carpenter's Gothic* takes full advantage of the resources of this genre to clarify the distinction between (and preferability of) ambiguity over absolutism and to warn against the dangers of mistaking fiction for fact.

The *Webster's New Collegiate Dictionary* (8th ed.) that Gaddis lambastes for inaccuracy each time Liz consults it (94, 248) gives three definitions of "fiction," each amply illustrated in *Carpenter's Gothic.* In fact, so many variations are played on this theme that it might be useful to resort to the sophomoric strategy of arguing directly from this dictionary's definitions, especially since Gaddis may have looked at them.

First Definition

1 a: something invented by the imagination or feigned; *specif:* an invented story <distinguish fact from~> b: fictitious literature (as novels or short stories) <a writer of~>.

Gaddis has always shown writers writing: in *The Recognitions,* Otto's struggles to concoct his play and Esme's to write poetry are dramatized, as is Jack Gibbs's work on *Agapē Agape* in *J R. Carpenter's Gothic* features two writers of fiction, both of whose works, however, blur the dictionary's distinction between fact and fiction. McCandless's novel is the object of Lester's extended scorn, partly because it follows the facts of the author's African experiences so closely that it doesn't merit the name fiction. The only aspects "invented" by McCandless seem to be slanderous aspersions (129), romantic self-aggrandizement (136–37), and pompous rhetoric *(passim).* Similarly, Liz's work in progress begins as autobiographical wishful thinking (63–64), but after McCandless's appearance begins to resemble a diary, reaching the point where her "fictional" account of an event is indistinguishable from the narrator's (cf. 163 and 257).

To modify Webster's definition, this is fact feigning as fiction, but perhaps a necessary sacrifice of "what really happens" to the "truth," that is, to something closer to how the authors experienced an event than a strict recital of the facts would allow. This is why Liz objects to the fanciful notion of setting up a mirror on Alpha Centauri in order to see through a telescope "what really happened" earlier in her life: "But you'd just see the outside though, wouldn't you" (153). Uninterested in aesthetic distance, Liz feels a writer's subjective sense of an experience is more important than the objective facts of the experience, a point she tries to impress upon McCandless, who prefers technical writing: "I'm talking about you, about what you know that nobody else knows because that's what writing's all about isn't it? I'm not a writer Mrs Booth I mean lots of people can write about all that, about grasshoppers and evolution and fossils I mean the things that only you know that's what I mean" (168). McCandless counters with "Maybe those are the things that you want to get away from," a position similar to Eliot's.[18] He made a better objection to Liz's point when he said earlier that too many writers "think if something happened to them that it's interesting because it happened to them" (158–59).

The aesthetic debate here concerning subjectivity vs. objectivity and the legitimacy of autobiography in fiction began in *The Recognitions,* where Hannah complained of Max's painting, "he has to learn that it isn't just having the experience that counts, it's knowing how to handle the experience" (*R* 184). In his third novel Gaddis enlivens the debate by showing how the autobiographical writer can confuse the invention of fiction with the invention of self, using fiction as an actor uses makeup to create a new persona, even a new life. For Liz, writing fiction offers "some hope of order restored, even that of a past itself in tatters, revised, amended, fabricated in fact from its very outset to reorder its unlikelihoods, what it all might have been" (247). Writing gives Liz access to what Billy calls her "real secret self" (193), the self Wyatt struggles to find in his quest for individuation, and the self Liz lost sight of "twenty, twenty five years away when it was all still, when things were still like you thought they were going to be" (154). Bibbs to her brother, Liz to her husband, Mrs. Booth to McCandless, "the redhead" to Lester, she resists this fragmentation of her identity by these men to insist "my name my name is Elizabeth" (166), the stuttered hesitation underscoring the difficulty she is having recovering the name of her true self from the men in her life.[19] Appropriately, her writing is conducted in secret; hidden in her drawer, her manuscript is a metonymy for her self, itself hidden so far from her husband that he is numbed when he comes across the manuscript after her death, written "in a hand he knew spelling little more than bread, onions, milk, chicken?" (257). Her failure to write parallels her failure to live, both captured in the flip title Gaddis briefly entertained for the novel: "That's All She Wrote."

Although McCandless completed and published his novel, it was published under a pseudonym; that, along with Lester's verdict ("rotten"), suggests his novel lacks the honesty and integrity he strives for in personal conduct. In an impressive apologia, he explains that one's life is a kind of fiction, to be crafted as carefully as a work of art:

—All that mattered was that I'd come through because I'd sworn to remember what really happened, that I'd never look back and let it become something romantic simply because I was young and a fool but I'd done it. I'd done it and I'd come out alive, and that's the way it's been ever since and maybe that's the hardest thing, harder than being sucked up in the clouds and meeting the Lord on judgment day or coming back with the Great Imam because *this fiction's all your own,* because you've spent your entire life at it who you are, and who you were when everything was possible, when you said that everything was still the way it was going to be no matter how badly we twist it around first chance we get and then make up a past to account for it. . . . (169; my italics)

If McCandless's fiction is indeed rotten, it is because he failed to construct it with the same fierce integrity that he constructed the "fiction" of his self. Like Hemingway's Frederic Henry, McCandless welcomes "facts proof against fine phrases that didn't mean anything" (228), but from Lester's quotations it sounds as though he preferred fine phrases when writing fiction. A better model would be Hemingway's reclusive contemporary Robinson Jeffers, parts of whose poem "Wise Men in Their Bad Hours" McCandless quotes on occasion (127, 161). Jeffers managed to put the same fierce integrity into his life as in his work, a synthesis McCandless apparently aims for but falls short of. If Liz's manuscript is a metonymy for her life, McCandless's study serves as his—a dusty, cobwebbed, smoke-filled room of books and papers that he continually tries to clean up, but where he manages only to create greater confusion and disorder. Alone, apparently friendless, estranged from his son and former wives, he sells out to the CIA for $16,000 and is last seen heading for the tropics, where the only way you know where you are is the disease you get (246). Again, failure in art means failure in life.

Second Definition

2: an assumption of a possibility as a fact irrespective of the question of its truth<a legal~>.

McCandless would argue that religions and metaphysical systems are possibilities (at best) assumed as facts by their followers, whose adherence to these fictions parodies an artist's quest for permanence in art:

—no no no, his voice as calming as the hand along her back, it was all just part of the eternal nonsense, where all the nonsense comes from about resurrection, transmigration, paradise, karma the whole damned lot. —It's all just fear he said, —you think of three quarters of the people in this country actually believing Jesus is alive in heaven? and two thirds of them that he's their ticket to eternal life? [. . .] just this panic at the idea of not existing so that joining that same Mormon wife and family in another life and you all come back together on judgment day, coming back with the Great Imam, coming back as the Dalai Lama choosing his parents in some Tibetan dung heap, coming back as anything —a dog, a mosquito, better than not coming back at all, the same panic wherever you look, any lunatic fiction to get through the night and the more farfetched the better, any evasion of the one thing in life that's absolutely inevitable [. . .] desperate fictions like the immortal soul and all these damned babies rushing around demanding to get born, or born again [. . .]. (157)

McCandless twice uses "fiction" here in the sense of Webster's second definition, as he does elsewhere: "talk about their deep religious convictions and that's what they are, they're convicts locked up in some shabby fiction doing life without parole and they want everybody else in prison with them" (186). The crucial difference is that literary and legal fictions are recognized as fictions; religious fictions are not. Fundamentalists, he implies, are like poor readers who first mistake a work of fiction for fact, then impose their literal-minded misreadings on others—at gunpoint if necessary. Not only are fundamentalists "doing more to degrade it taking every damned word in it literally than any militant atheist could ever hope to," he fumes, but they don't even recognize the contradictions in the Bible any attentive reader would note (134, 136). The status of fiction and the validity of interpretation thus become more than academic matters for literary theorists; if the fundamentalist misreadings of sacred fictions prevail, aided by politicians misreading their constitutions, Armageddon will put an end to all fictions.

All the world's a text, Gaddis implies, and all the men and women merely readers. In *Carpenter's Gothic* leaves from a tree become leaves from a book within half a sentence (197), and bed sheets still damp from Liz and McCandless's lovemaking become in the next paragraph sheets of paper that will become damp with ink to describe the event (198). Gaddis's characters are forced to read the world around them despite the general illegibility of that "text": the clock is untrustworthy, the newspapers unreliable, the dictionary inaccurate, even words misleading: Liz and Madame Socrate founder on the French homonyms *salle* and *sale* (26; cf. the confusion over *sale* and *salé* in *The Recognitions*, 943), the two meanings of "morgue'" confuse her (225), and half-listening to the radio's account of "a thrilling rescue operation by the Coast Guard" (116) Liz is puzzled the next day about a "thrilling rescue by postcard" (158). Even single letters cause confusion, leading Paul to think Billy doesn't even know how to spell Buddha (85). Ambiguity haunts the simplest words.

Gaddis's most brilliant dramatization of the vagaries of interpretation recalls the doubloon Melville's Ahab nails to the mainmast of the *Pequod*. Anxious to give a distracted Liz "the big picture" of the various religious and political complications in which he is enmeshed, Paul draws a diagram showing these various groups and the interactions between them. The first to interpret this diagram, after Paul, is the narrator, who offers humorous asides on the shapes that grow beneath Paul's hand (the administration is represented by "something vaguely phallic"), cruel social innuendo ("all his blacks down here . . . a smudge unconnected to anything"), and ending with the fanciful observation that Paul's flow-chart arrows "darkened the page like the skies that day over Crécy" (100–1, 107). When McCandless comes across this drawing, he only sees the scribblings of a child (118), as does Lester when he first sees it (124). But looking at it again (147), Lester realizes it does indeed resemble the battle of Cressy (as he pronounces it), though he needs to adjust the figures in the drawing somewhat, much like a critic pounding the square peg of a thesis into the round hole of a text. In addition to foreshadowing the militaristic results of the Teakell–Ude–Grimes cartel—Armageddon promises to be the last use of firepower as the battle of Crécy was the first—and exposing the childishness of it all, this example highlights the dangers of interpretation that surround all the characters, none of whom commands a vantage point from which "the big picture" can be seen, but each of whom believes he or she holds the right interpretation of the text. A fable for critics.

Gaddis's own text has already generated the same kind of contradictory readings; with at least seven types of ambiguity in it, this is not surprising, though a few of the readings are. The novel struck most reviewers as savagely pessimistic, but one felt Gaddis "makes his optimism plain enough on the surface. The book ends with no period, indicating continuation. It hints at reincarnation, if only as a fly."[20] No comment. More than one reviewer accused McCandless of being mad. There are a few teasing innuendos to that effect, but his "madness" is more likely one more of the deceptions inherent in Carpenter Gothic, one made by linking Mrs. McCandless's remark that her former husband spent time in a hospital (250) with Lester's taunting question "you used to say I'd rather have a bottle in front of me than a frontal lobotomy where'd you get that, that's somebody else too isn't it because you've got one" (140). But the clever line is only a gag from a Tom Waits song of the mid-seventies, and Lester's accusation is strictly metaphoric; he goes on to say "the figures on lung cancer right in front of you like the facts staring those primates square in the face out there choking on Genesis and you say it's just a statistical parallel and light another." Gaddis realizes (if McCandless doesn't) that the choice between the truth and what really happens is not as easy to make as McCandless pretends it is, but rather owes more to the instinct to cling to what he later castigates as "any lunatic fiction to get through the night and the more farfetched the better, any evasion of the one thing in life that's absolutely inevitable" (157). Faced with the inevitability of death, McCandless panics as easily as any fundamentalist, but that is hardly a sign of madness; the reader should not be misled by talk of lobotomies and lunacy into thinking McCandless was in that hospital for anything worse than malaria (152). Yet another critic has suggested that Paul and Edie team up to murder Liz![21] Although there is some question who is telephoning as she expires—both Paul and McCandless know the ringing code (246)—there can be no question Liz is alone, hitting her head on the kitchen table as she goes down. Yet see how I resist the ambiguity, insisting on certainty; it's a hard habit to break.

Third Definition

3: the action of feigning or of creating with the imagination

This activity thus emerges as both constructive and destructive in *Carpenter's Gothic,* an action that can be used for self-realization or misused for self-delusion. At one extreme is the "paranoid sentimental fiction" of the American South (224) or the "serviceable fiction" of the African Masai that justifies their stealing cattle from other tribes because of "their ancient belief that all the cattle in the world belong to them" (121). At the other extreme are such fictions as *Heart of Darkness*—which McCandless declares "an excellent thing," even though Liz ascribes it to Faulkner and confuses it with Styron's *Lie Down in Darkness* (158)—and Jeffers's "Wise Men in Their Bad Hours." Gaddis's characters largely misuse fiction and are more often seen feigning than creating anything worthwhile. But Gaddis himself faced and overcame the same problems in writing this novel, one that exemplifies the proper use of fiction and achieves the ideal set in the concluding lines of the Jeffers poem, the lines McCandless never quotes, perhaps because his creator has reserved them for himself:

> Ah, grasshoppers,
> Death's a fierce meadowlark: but to die having made
> Something more equal to the centuries
> Than muscle and bone, is mostly to shed weakness.
> The mountains are dead stone, the people
> Admire or hate their stature, their insolent quietness,
> The mountains are not softened nor troubled
> And a few dead men's thoughts have the same temper.

McCandless's Carpenter Gothic has stood ninety years, he boasts; Gaddis's *Carpenter's Gothic* should stand at least as long.

Chapter Seven

In the American Grain

With *Carpenter's Gothic* it becomes clear that America has always been Gaddis's great subject. The theme of personal failure he identified for his lectures on American literature is subsumed in his own work by the larger theme of the failure of America itself. Throughout his work, as in much of Jack Kerouac's, there is a feeling of bitter disappointment at America's failure to fulfill its potential, to live up to the magnificent expectations held for the New World ever since Columbus declared it the Terrestrial Paradise predicted by Scripture. Instead, we find a country in the first novel so immersed in counterfeit it can no longer tell the difference between the genuine and the fake, except to prefer the latter; in the second, people talking themselves to death in a country running down from cultural entropy; and in the third, America at its last gasp, facing the yellow dead-end sign planted at the foot of the novel's first page. "It's too late to try to . . . " Liz murmurs at one point, only to be interrupted by Paul's more final "Too late" (216).

Carpenter's Gothic, like *The Great Gatsby* sixty years before it, suggests that it is too late to reverse the tide, to restore the promise of the American dream. In fact, as McCandless points out in a valedictory speech late in the novel, the dream has become a nightmare:

—Two hundred years building this great bastion of middle class values, fair play, pay your debts, fair pay for honest work, two hundred years that's about all it is, progress, improvement everywhere, what's worth doing is worth doing well and they ["the new generation"] find out that's the most dangerous thing of all, all our grand solutions turn into their nightmares. Nuclear energy to bring cheap power everywhere and all they hear is radiation threats and what in hell to do with the waste. Food for the millions and they're back eating organic sprouts and stone ground flour because everything else is poisonous additives, pesticides poisoning the earth, poisoning the rivers the oceans and the conquest of space turns into military satellites and high technology where the only metaphor we've given them is the neutron bomb and the only news is today's front page. . . . (230)

The only survivors in *Carpenter's Gothic*—Paul, Edie, and the smirking neighborhood kids—hint at an even bleaker future, dominated by moral jackals and hyenas. (Lawyers are reportedly the subject of Gaddis's next novel.)

Even though Gaddis's novels have contemporary settings, he avoids the historical amnesia McCandless complains of in his last line by anchoring each of his novels in specific aspects of the American past: in *The Recognitions,* the Calvinist tradition of New England, nineteenth-century Protestantism, twentieth-century expatriation, and even Columbus's voyage of discovery; in *J R,* late–nineteenth-century social and educational reform movements, robber barons and unregulated capitalism, and the Protestant work ethic of Benjamin Franklin and Horatio Alger; in *Carpenter's Gothic,* the anti-intellectual religious tradition that has bedeviled America every other generation since the Great Awakening in the 1700s and the legacy of the South's defeat in the Civil War, which created "this cradle of stupidity where they get patriotism and Jesus all mixed together because that's the religion of losers" (224). Although Gaddis avoids the kind of historical set pieces favored by Barth and Pynchon, he joins them in trying to correct that fault William Carlos Williams complained of to Valéry Larbaud in his documentary history *In the American Grain:* "It is an extraordinary phenomenon that Americans have lost the sense, being made up as we are, that what we are has its origin in what *the nation* in the past has been; that there is a source in AMERICA for everything we think or do."[1]

Gaddis's work is also anchored in America's literary traditions. The criticism of puritan/fundamentalist religion in his first and third novels looks back obviously to Hawthorne's *Scarlet Letter* and Melville's harsh critiques of Christianity, but also to Mark Twain (Christian Science as well as mainstream Christianity) and to such works as Harold Frederic's *Damnation of Theron Ware* and Sinclair Lewis's *Elmer Gantry.* Gaddis's use of apocalypse is firmly rooted in an American tradition that R. W. B. Lewis has traced back to Melville's *Confidence-Man,* which he considers

the recognizable and awe-inspiring ancestor of several subsequent works of fiction in America: Mark Twain's *The Man That Corrupted Hadleyburg* and *The Mysterious Stranger,* for example; and more recently, Nathanael West's *The Day of the Locust,* Faulkner's *The Hamlet,* Ralph Ellison's *Invisible Man,* William Gaddis' *The Recognitions,* John Barth's *The Sot-Weed Factor,* Thomas Pynchon's [*sic*] *V.* Melville bequeathed to those works—in very differing proportions—

the vision of an apocalypse that is no less terrible for being enormously comic, the self-extinction of a world characterized by deceit and thronging with imposters and masqueraders[. . .].[2]

Gaddis's satire of the abuses of capitalism in *J R* joins a long tradition of American antibusiness novels running from William Dean Howells's *The Rise of Silas Lapham* through Theodore Dreiser's Cowperwood trilogy, more Sinclair Lewis (*Babbitt* and *Dodsworth*), to contemporary novels by Vonnegut and Heller. In fact, John Brooks grumbles that Gaddis may have killed off the genre: "With 'J R' we have the American business novel, as to form, coming to the sort of dead end that the novel in general came to with James Joyce."[3] I prefer to see *J R* as capping that genre and disproving Henry Nash Smith's complaint that "serious writers seem unable to take an interest in a system of values based on economic assumptions."[4]

Finally, Gaddis's allegiance to the comic tradition in American literature should not be overlooked, despite the gravity of his themes. As Lewis points out, even the Apocalypse can be enormously comic, and all of Gaddis's work is animated by a comic brio that adds a kind of desperate hilarity to his grim themes. From the Marx Brothers shenanigans in *J R* to more subtle examples of learned wit, Gaddis's novels, like Janus, wear the masks of comedy and tragedy simultaneously, a strategy that prevents them from becoming ponderous or depressing, and one that relies on the comic as much for its entertainment value as for its philosophical stance. Gaddis's favorite review of *J R*, for example, appeared not in any of the prestigious New York journals or literary quarterlies but in the "provincial" *Cleveland Plain-Dealer*, whose reviewer admitted: "If Gaddis is a moralist, he is also a master of satire and humor. *J R* is a devastatingly funny book. Reading it, I laughed loudly and unashamedly in public places, and at home, more than once, I saw my small children gather in consternation as tears of laughter ran down my face."[5] Critics may consider that inconsequential praise, but Gaddis's fellow writers would be green with envy.

In fact, writers rather than critics were the first to recognize Gaddis's enormous achievement, as witnessed by the surprisingly large number of contemporary novels in which Gaddis and/or his novels appear. His early association with the Beats led to his becoming the model for Harry Lees in Chandler Brossard's *Who Walk in Darkness* (1952) and for Harold Sand in Jack Kerouac's *The Subterraneans* (1958). (In exchange,

Gaddis lifted a few lines from William Burroughs's *Junkie* for his own demi-Beat novel.[6]) David Markson, acquainted with the Beats but closer in spirit to his mentor Malcolm Lowry, refers to *The Recognitions* and parodies Gaddis's style of dialogue in his detective novel *Epitaph for a Tramp* (1959). He has continued to refer to him in other works: the opening line of *The Recognitions* is quoted (in a chapter of opening lines) in his delightful *Springer's Progress* (1977) and Gaddis flits through the memory of mad Kate a dozen times in Markson's last novel, *Wittgenstein's Mistress* (1988). *The Recognitions* appears on the bookshelf of the protagonist of Richard Horn's innovative novel *Encyclopedia* (1969), and *J R* is named and amusingly imitated in John Sladek's science fiction novel *Roderick* (1980). More recently, Gaddis's friend Stanley Elkin included in his novel *The Magic Kingdom* (1985) an eight-year-old geriatric named Charles Mudd-Gaddis—a name that gave Gaddis some puzzled bemusement—and an editor named Virginia Wrappers ("the guardian of standards") in Charles Simmons's *jeu d'esprit The Belles Lettres Papers* (1987) includes Gaddis on her list of the twenty-five best writers in America.

Gaddis's stylistic influence on contemporary writers is more difficult to access. His general contribution to black humor and the revival of Menippean satire was noted in my first chapter, but his direct influence on particular writers is arguable. Some novels, like Sladek's *Roderick* and Markson's *Going Down* (1970), show unmistakable signs of influence, explicitly in Sladek's case, implicitly in Markson's brilliant novel.[7] Other novelists have testified to Gaddis's influence on their own work: Joseph McElroy has acknowledged the role *The Recognitions* played in shaping his first novel, *A Smuggler's Bible* (1966),[8] and Don DeLillo has praised Gaddis "for extending the possibilities of the novel by taking huge risks and making great demands on his readers."[9] Harry Mathews told me he modeled the title of his first novel, *The Conversions* (1962), on that of Gaddis's first novel, though he didn't actually read *The Recognitions* until sometime in the 1970s. Robert Shea reportedly had *The Recognitions* in mind when he wrote the *Illuminatus!* trilogy with Robert Anton Wilson (1975), but the result more resembles Pynchon's paranoid fictions than Gaddis's. Some of Donald Barthelme's dialogue-stories resemble pages from *J R,* but the resemblance may be as misleading as that with Gilbert Sorrentino's dialogue-novel *Crystal Vision* (1981), which was inspired not by *J R* but by William Carlos Williams's *A Novelette*. Gaddis's novels have also earned the praise of

Stanley Elkin, William H. Gass, Paul West, and David Foster Wallace, but it would be safer to say these novelists, along with Barth and Coover, share affinities with Gaddis rather than show his influence.

The novelist most often linked with Gaddis by way of both influence and affinity is Thomas Pynchon. *V.* especially has struck a number of critics as reminiscent of *The Recognitions* in many ways: structurally, both consist of dual narrative lines that occasionally intersect; both indict masculine principles for a variety of modern ills and feature motherless sons attempting to restore the balance by aligning themselves with feminine principles; both alternate between Greenwich Village scenes and European locations; both are widely allusive, often to the same authors; both use comical names for some of their characters; and so on. Similarly, Gaddis's *J R* resembles *Gravity's Rainbow* in some ways: both often allude to Wagner and Weber; both hold Western economic policies chiefly responsible for the deteriorating quality of modern life; both indict American and European exploitation of Third World nations; and both make demands upon the reader unheard of since *Finnegans Wake*. With the publication of *Carpenter's Gothic*, the pattern seemed complete: several reviewers noted Gaddis now had a counterpart to Pynchon's *Crying of Lot 49*, another short work featuring a neglected housewife haunted by ambiguities.

But in an essay on this particular topic, I found that the similarities between their works looked more like a case of what Leni Pökler in *Gravity's Rainbow*, using electrical imagery, would describe as "'Parallel, not series.'"[10] The resemblances between *V.* and *The Recognitions* are of the duplicitous sort that led many reviewers to assume Gaddis's novel was an imitation of Joyce's *Ulysses*, and the thematic similarities between the later novels obscure the pronounced tonal differences and cultural allegiances that separate the two. As a recent Pynchon critic has written, Gaddis's work "lacks Pynchon's delight in the varied, zany, countercultural aspects of popular culture. It also lacks Pynchon's scientific and occult interests, his brilliant colloquial style (though Gaddis is a better and thoroughly damning mimic of spoken colloquial voices), and Pynchon's warmth."[11] What can be said, however, is that Pynchon is one of the very few rivals Gaddis has among contemporary novelists in the English-speaking world.

Gaddis's body of work may have a superficial resemblance to Pynchon's, but it displays an organic form all its own. Joseph McElroy likened it to the contracting universe: "the big bang" with the thousand-page first novel, "and the slow evolution out of that" with *J R*, "then down to what is almost a paradigm, or a *pensée*," *Carpenter's Gothic*.[12] But I prefer to see the three novels as cultural soundings corresponding to the three ages of adulthood: youth and expansive idealism in *The Recognitions*; middle age and evasive idealism under siege in *J R*; and the beginning of laconic old age with idealism lost in *Carpenter's Gothic*. Even though each of Gaddis's novels teems with characters of all ages, these three ages determine the principal moral viewpoint in each and the darkening pessimistic outlook. In either case, Gaddis's work reveals an organic continuity elegant in its progression, relentless in its engagement with the major issues of the time, and unique in contemporary American literature.

Postscript: A Legal Fiction

In 1987 Gaddis published the first excerpt from his next novel, a short fiction in the form of a legal opinion entitled "Szyrk v. Village of Tatamount et al."[13] A further argument for McElroy's thesis, this fiction represents the most compact presentation yet of Gaddis's characteristic themes and parodic techniques. It takes its premise from an incident in *J R*: the huge steel sculpture *Cyclone 7* that entraps a boy near the end of *J R* (671–72) has its counterpart in a small town in Virginia, where it entraps a dog this time. Its sculptor, a SoHo artist named Szyrk (pronounced "Zrk" as in "Srskić" [*J R* 557–58]), files for a temporary restraining order to prevent the local fire department from injuring his work in its attempt to free the dog. The fiction consists of Judge Crease's decision to grant the sculptor a preliminary injunction to supersede the temporary order.

All of Gaddis's characteristic themes and concerns are here: the artist at odds with the community, the validity of art, the media's role in shaping public opinion, the intellectual poverty of the South, chauvinistic patriotism, political chicanery, and of course the Byzantine workings of the law. The story is a tour de force in legal wit of the kind used by Rabelais, Swift, Sterne, and Melville, as well as by Gaddis himself. *J R*, it will be remembered, opens with the attorney Coen weaving a web of legal fictions around the Bast sisters with such findings as "in the case of a child conceived or born in wedlock, it must be shown that the husband of the mother could not possibly have been the father of the child" (11) reminiscent of Walter Shandy's finding "That the mother was not kin to her child" by a similar mazy path of legal quibbling. Writing in 1951 of the disappearance of this sort of learned wit, D. W. Jefferson noted, "Fewer people need to go to law today, so we are all less legally minded; [. . .] The community has benefited from these reforms, but a theme for wit has been lost."[14] Gaddis has recovered this theme for our litigious society by means of his unmatched gift for parody, rendering an opinion in a brilliant display of legal discourse complete with citations and spacious learning. (It is not surprising that, asked what field he would have entered had he not become a writer, Gaddis answered, "The law."[15]) The orotund periods and Olympian ironies of Judge Crease's language do not conceal a crusty outlook of the sort one expects from Gaddis's older protagonists. Crease takes a dim view of Szyrk's postmodernist work, for example—his references to Shakespeare, Donatello, and Eliot (among others) define his artistic sensibility—and he passes judgment on self-referential art, denigrating

the theory that in having become self-referential art is in itself theory without which it has no more substance than Sir Arthur Eddington's famous step "on a swarm of flies," here present in further exhibits by plaintiff drawn from prestigious art publications and highly esteemed critics in the lay press, where they make their livings, recommending his sculptural creation in terms of slope, tangent, acceleration, force, energy, and similar abstract extravagancies serving only a corresponding self-referential confrontation of language with language and thereby, in reducing language itself to theory, rendering it a mere plaything, which exhibits the court finds frivolous. (46–47)

But at the same time holding "the conviction that risk of ridicule, of attracting defamatory attentions from his colleagues and even raucous demonstrations by an outraged public have ever been and remain the foreseeable lot of the serious artist" (49–50), Crease gives the back of his hand to critics and complainants alike and finds in favor of the plaintiff with one of the most eloquent defenses of venturesome art in our time. In so doing, the learned judge also gives conclusive evidence, if more were needed, of the inquisitorial art of William Gaddis.

Notes and References

Chapter One

1. George Stade, review of *Ratner's Star* by Don DeLillo, *New York Times Book Review*, 20 June 1976, 7.

2. Frank D. McConnell, reader's report on Steven Moore's *A Reader's Guide to William Gaddis's "The Recognitions,"* 31 July 1980.

3. *Contemporary Authors*, ed. James M. Ethridge, Barbara Kopala, and Carolyn Riley, vol. 19/20 (Detroit: Gale Research, 1968), 135.

4. *The Recognitions* (1955; reprint, New York: Penguin, 1985), 240; hereafter cited in the text, abbreviated *R* when necessary. Because Gaddis uses ellipses extensively, my ellipses are bracketed; for consistency, I follow this practice in all cited material.

5. Interview with Miriam Berkley, 17 June 1985. A condensed version of this interview was published in *Publishers Weekly*, 12 July 1985, 56–57, but all of my quotations are from the unedited transcript, with a few corrections supplied by Gaddis.

6. John Aldridge, review of *J R, Saturday Review*, 4 October 1975, 27.

7. Frederick Karl, "American Fictions: The Mega-Novel," *Conjunctions* 7 (1985):248.

8. *Carpenter's Gothic* (1985; reprint, New York: Penguin, 1986), 59, 64; hereafter cited in the text.

9. John Kuehl and Steven Moore, "An Interview with William Gaddis," *Review of Contemporary Fiction* 2, no. 2 (Summer 1982):4.

10. Malcolm Bradbury, *Writers in Conversation 13: William Gaddis* (London: Institute of Contemporary Arts, 1986). Videocassette distributed by the Rowland Collection, Northbrook, Ill.

11. Further biographical details are available in the introduction to *In Recognition of William Gaddis*, ed. John Kuehl and Steven Moore (Syracuse, N.Y.: Syracuse University Press, 1984), and in Louis Auchincloss, "Recognizing Gaddis," *New York Times Magazine*, 15 November 1987, 36, 38, 41, 54, 58.

12. Cynthia Ozick, review of *Carpenter's Gothic, New York Times Book Review*, 7 July 1985, 1.

13. Tony Tanner, review of the Avon reprint of *The Recognitions, New York Times Book Review*, 14 July 1974, 28.

14. Frederick Karl, "Gaddis: A Tribune of the Fifties," in Kuehl and Moore, *In Recognition*, 176.

15. *Letters of Delmore Schwartz*, ed. Robert Philips (Princeton: Ontario Review Press, 1984), 298.

16. Berkley interview.

17. Letter to Jean [?] Howes, 8 March 1972, quoted in Grace Eckley, "Exorcising the Demon Forgery, or the Forging of Pure Gold in Gaddis's *Recognitions*," in *Literature and the Occult*, ed. Luanne Frank (Arlington: University of Texas Press, 1977), 125. Gaddis's reference is to Bernard Benstock, "On William Gaddis: In Recognition of James Joyce," *Wisconsin Studies in Contemporary Literature* 6 (Summer 1965):177–89. David Markson was responsible for introducing Benstock to Gaddis in the early sixties; though impressed by *The Recognitions*, Benstock felt only by linking Gaddis to Joyce could he get his essay published.

18. Anselm twice refers to the critic in the green wool shirt as a "three-time psychoanaloser" (*R* 183, 453). In *Finnegans Wake*, Yawn boasts, "I can psoakoonaloose myself any time I want" (New York: Viking, 1939), 522.

19. Letter dated 3 June 1975.

20. William H. Gass, "Some Snapshots from the Soviet Zone," *Kenyon Review* 8, no. 4 (Fall 1986):15.

21. Edward Wasiolek, "Tolstoy's 'The Death of Ivan Ilytch' and Jamesian Fictional Imperatives," in *Tolstoy: A Collection of Critical Essays*, ed. Ralph E. Matlaw (Englewood Cliffs, N.J.: Prentice-Hall, 1967), 154.

22. Marie-Rose Logan and Tomasz Mirkowicz, "'If You Bring Nothing to a Work . . . ': An Interview with William Gaddis," unpublished translation by Julita Wroniak of "'Kto do utworu przychodzi z niczym . . .': Z Williamem Gaddisem rozmawiają," *Literatura na Świecie* 1/150 (1984).

23. Letter dated 28 February 1961; the quotation from Lowry that follows is from an unpublished letter to Markson dated 22 February 1957.

24. "The Rush for Second Place," *Harper's*, April 1981, 32. This essay, based on his Bard lectures, is the source for most of the titles that follow.

25. D. H. Lawrence, *Studies in Classic American Literature* (1923; reprint, New York: Viking, 1964), 47.

26. "How Does the State Imagine?" 48th International PEN Congress, New York, 13 January 1986.

27. Postcard to me postmarked 6 August 1982.

28. Milton Rugoff, review of *The Recognitions*, *New York Herald Tribune Book Review*, 13 March 1955, 6.

29. Gilbert Sorrentino, *Something Said* (San Francisco: North Point Press, 1984), 209. See also Sorrentino's review of Gaddis's *J R* in the same volume (180–83).

30. To see how little J R has learned, see Gaddis's amusing update, "Trickle-Up Economics: J R Goes to Washington," *New York Times Book Review*, 25 October 1987, 29.

31. Logan and Mirkowicz interview.

32. Aldridge, review of *J R*, 30.

33. Rust Hills, "Don't Everybody Talk at Once! (The *Esquire* Literary

Survey)," *Esquire,* August 1986, 100.

34. Leslie A. Fiedler, *Love and Death in the American Novel,* rev. ed. (New York: Stein and Day, 1966), 432.

35. "Szyrk v. Village of Tatamount et al.," *New Yorker,* 12 October 1987, 50.

Chapter Two

1. Stephen Spender, "Introduction," *Under the Volcano* by Malcolm Lowry (New York: Lippincott, 1965), xi–xii.

2. Kafka's reaction to Tolstoy's *Resurrection,* quoted in Ronald Hayman's *Kafka: A Biography* (New York: Oxford University Press, 1982), 255.

3. Documentation of Gaddis's use of all these sources can be found in Steven Moore, *Reader's Guide to William Gaddis's "The Recognitions"* (Lincoln: University of Nebraska Press, 1982).

4. See Jack Green's scathing review of Gaddis's reviewers, "fire the bastards!" *newspaper* 12–14 (1962).

5. Harold Beaver, "Introduction," *Moby-Dick* by Herman Melville (New York: Penguin, 1972), 26.

6. T. S. Eliot, *"Ulysses,* Order, and Myth," in *Selected Prose of T. S. Eliot,* ed. Frank Kermode (London: Faber & Faber, 1975), 177.

7. Carl G. Jung, *The Integration of the Personality,* trans. Stanley M. Dell (New York: Farrar & Rinehart, 1939), 69.

8. Robert Graves, *The White Goddess* (New York: Creative Age Press, 1948), 154. The quotation that follows is on p. 76.

9. Ibid., 261. When Wyatt examines the dead Recktall Brown he seizes the exposed ankle, seeking a pulse, and mutters, "Yes, there's where they nailed the wren, there's where they nailed up . . . " (683). "He was so kind and fatherly" Wyatt said earlier with drunken sentimentality (376), indicating Brown too acts in Wyatt's Oedipal drama.

10. Sir James George Frazer, *The Golden Bough,* abridged ed. (New York: Macmillan, 1922), 193.

11. Jung, *Integration,* 34.

12. See especially Joseph S. Salemi's "To Soar in Atonement: Art as Expiation in Gaddis' *The Recognitions"* and Christopher Knight's "Flemish Art and Wyatt's Quest for Redemption in William Gaddis' *The Recognitions,"* both in Kuehl and Moore, *In Recognition.*

13. Aniela Jaffé, *Apparitions and Precognition* (New Hyde Park, N.Y.: University Books, 1963), 154, 32, 31–32.

14. Wallace Stevens, "The Comedian as the Letter C," *The Palm at the End of the Mind,* ed. Holly Stevens (New York: Knopf, 1971), 65.

15. Ludwig Wittgenstein, *Remarks on Frazer's "Golden Bough,"* trans. A. C. Miles (Retford, England: Brynmill, 1979), 5e.

16. Miriam Fuchs, "'Il miglior fabbro': Gaddis' Debt to T. S. Eliot," in Kuehl and Moore, *In Recognition*, 99.

17. Heracles is "waving a piece of bread" when Gwyon comes for him—recalling the Eucharist—and the description of Heracles's burial place (54–55) is taken from the Gospels (Matt. 27:60, Mark 16:4). Wyatt feels nails are being driven into his feet when he attempts to walk, recalling the Crucifixion itself.

18. The source of Aunt May's harangue is Catholic apologist Denis de Rougemont's *The Devil's Share,* trans. Haakon Chevalier (New York: Pantheon, 1944), 29, 38. Her comments, then, cannot be dismissed as simply the personal outrage of a soured Calvinist. The injunctions against pictorial art in Hebrew and Moslem traditions spring from the same belief that creation is a divine perogative.

19. Quoted in David Koenig's "The Writing of *The Recognitions,"* in Kuehl and Moore, *In Recognition*, 23.

20. In his study *The Heretics,* Walter Nigg writes: "In his struggle against the declining morality of Roman Christendom, Pelagius made the significant observation that the degeneration could not be ascribed to the decay of the Empire, which at that time was undergoing its last agony. Moral decline, Pelagius held, was indirectly fostered by the doctrine which stressed man's redemption through Christ too exclusively and ignored man's own efforts" (trans. Richard and Clara Winston [New York: Knopf, 1962], 133–34).

21. Montague Summers, ed. and trans., *The Malleus Maleficarum* by Heinrich Kramer and James Sprenger (1928; reprint, New York: Dover, 1971), 46b, note.

22. Jung, *Integration,* 73, 106.

23. The Town Carpenter echoes Thoreau, of course: see *Walden,* chap. 2. Charles Banning considers the Town Carpenter "a haunting 'reincarnation' of Thoreau" ("The Time of Our Time: William Gaddis, John Hawkes and Thomas Pynchon," Ph.D. diss., State University of New York at Buffalo, 1977, 154 n.24).

24. Robert Graves, *Difficult Questions, Easy Answers* (Garden City, N.Y.: Doubleday, 1971), 122.

25. Jung, *Integration,* 79.

26. Wyatt/Stephen tells Ludy, "They're waiting for me now," presumably referring to Pastora and the child she's expecting. "—Her earrings, he said, —that's where these are for" (900; cf. the child in the epigraph to this chapter). See Koenig for Gaddis's original intentions regarding a daughter (Kuehl and Moore, *In Recognition*, 24–25), and cf. *R* 127 for Wyatt's long-standing interest in a daughter.

27. Both Latin forms are given in the *Oxford Dictionary of Quotations,* Gaddis's probable source. His other borrowings from the *ODQ* are noted in Steven Moore, "Additional Sources for William Gaddis's *The Recognitions,"*

American Notes & Queries 22 (March/April 1984): 113–14, with this correction: the text Gaddis used was the first edition, sixth printing (1949), not the second edition of 1953.

Chapter Three

1. Koenig, in Kuehl and Moore, *In Recognition,* 28.
2. Quoted in Peter [now David] Koenig, "'Splinters from the Yew Tree': A Critical Study of William Gaddis' *The Recognitions,"* Ph.D. diss., New York University, 1971, 100.
3. J. B. Leishman's notes to *The Duino Elegies* by Rainer Maria Rilke, trans. Leishman and Stephen Spender (New York: Norton, 1939), 87–88. This is the translation Gaddis quotes from.
4. William Gaddis, review of *More Die of Heartbreak* by Saul Bellow, *New York Times Book Review,* 24 May 1987, 1.
5. John Seelye, "Dryad in a Dead Oak Tree: The Incognito in *The Recognitions,"* in Kuehl and Moore, *In Recognition,* 72.
6. For Gaddis's use of Ibsen, see Steven Moore, *"Peer Gynt* and *The Recognitions,"* ibid., 81–91.
7. Fiedler, *Love and Death,* 314.
8. J. Huizinga, *The Waning of the Middle Ages,* trans. F. Hopman (London: Edward Arnold, 1924), 240; the Van Eyck painting is reproduced opposite p. 141.
9. Koenig, "'Splinters from the Yew Tree,'" 93.
10. William Butler Yeats, "Crazy Jane Talks with the Bishop" (1933).
11. Merton's *Seven Storey Mountain* (1948) may be a model for Anselm's career in some details; the reviews of Anselm's book on p. 935 are quite similar to the ones Merton's book received.
12. James Joyce, *Ulysses* (1922; reprint, New York: Random, 1986), 170.
13. Huizinga, *Waning,* v.
14. Harold H. Watts, "William Gaddis," in *Great Writers of the English Language: Novelists and Prose Writers,* ed. James Vinson (New York: St. Martin's Press, 1979), 434.
15. Johan Thielemans has perceptively analyzed Gaddis's party chat in "The Energy of an Absence: Perfection as Useful Fiction in the Novels of Gaddis and Sorrentino," in *Critical Angles: European Views of Contemporary American Literature,* ed. Marc Chénetier (Carbondale: Southern Illinois University Press, 1986), 105–24.

Chapter Four

1. *R* 741 and *J R* (1975; reprint, New York: Penguin, 1985), 719; hereafter cited in the text. "Nobody Grew But the Business" is also the title of a prepublication extract from *J R* that appeared in *Harper's* in 1975.

2. Norbert Wiener, *The Human Use of Human Beings,* rev. ed. (1954; reprint, New York: Avon, 1967), 25.

3. This is actually from a review of *Carpenter's Gothic,* which is written in the same style as *J R,* but it echoes similar complaints made of the second novel: Bruce Allen, "Gaddis's Dense Satire of Greed Is Often Amusing, Mostly Confusing," *Christian Science Monitor,* 17 September 1985, 26.

4. Carl Malmgren, "William Gaddis's *J R:* The Novel of Babel," *Review of Contemporary Fiction* 2, no. 2 (Summer 1982): 10–11.

5. D. Keith Mano, "Gaddis's House Rules," *Harper's Bookletter* 2, no. 6 (27 October 1975):4.

6. Shlomith Rimmon-Kenan, *Narrative Fiction: Contemporary Poetics* (New York: Metheun, 1983), 45.

7. Richard Bulliet, letter to the editor, *Columbia,* January 1983, 36.

8. If the chronology I once constructed for *J R* were valid, the first third of the novel would occupy about two weeks, the following thirds about a week each: see my "Chronological Difficulties in the Novels of William Gaddis," *Critique* 22, no. 1 (1980):88–89. Although I now see that this time frame is too brief—Gaddis later wrote me "the novel's technique demanded compressing time so, I was afraid I'd be called on it but no one did" (1 June 1986)—the proportions are about right: Gaddis apparently intended the first third to occupy a month or so, the second and third a few weeks each. Closer attention to other details in the novel suggests it takes place in the fall of 1972—not 1974, as in my article—though the absence of any reference to the presidential election that year makes even this date suspect.

9. Stanley P. Friedman, "Five Novelists at Work: A Grapeshot Interview," *Book World,* 10 March 1968, 10.

10. Here as elsewhere (289, 585), Gibbs quotes from Benjamin Jowett's translation of Aristotle's *Politics.*

11. Max Weber, *The Protestant Ethic and the Spirit of Capitalism,* trans. Talcott Parsons (New York: Scribner's, 1958), 181. For Gaddis's familiarity with Weber's work, see "The Rush for Second Place."

12. Friedrich Engels, *The Origin of the Family, Private Property, and the State* (1884), quoted in *The Marx-Engels Reader,* 2nd ed., ed. Robert C. Tucker (New York: Norton, 1978), 748—a concept, Engels points out, that can be found in *The Communist Manifesto.*

13. Philip Rahv, *Image and Idea: Fourteen Essays on Literary Themes* (Norfolk, Conn.: New Directions, 1949), 122–23.

14. See Weber, *The Protestant Ethic,* 168–70, but also Wyatt's Aunt May (*R* 34).

15. Weber, *The Protestant Ethic,* 166.

16. Wiener, *Human Use,* 41.

17. Ibid., 84.

18. Leslie A. Fiedler, *No! in Thunder* (Boston: Beacon, 1960), 251, 290.

19. Weber, *The Protestant Ethic,* 181.

20. Sándor Ferenczi, "The Ontogenesis of the Interest in Money," in *The Psychoanalysis of Money,* ed. Ernest Bornemann (New York: Urizen, 1976), 81–90.

21. An excellent discussion of the waste motif can be found in Thomas LeClair's "William Gaddis, *J R,* & the Art of Excess," *Modern Fiction Studies* 27 (Winter 1981–82):591–93.

22. Weber, *The Protestant Ethic,* 124.

23. Johan Thielemans, "Art as Redemption of Trash: Bast and Friends in Gaddis's *J R,"* in Kuehl and Moore, *In Recognition,* 144.

24. Robert Donington, *Wagner's "Ring" and Its Symbols,* 3rd ed. (New York: St. Martin's Press, 1974), 52.

25. Norman O. Brown, *Life Against Death: The Psychoanalytic Meaning of History* (Middletown, Conn.: Wesleyan University Press, 1959), 238. Brown is summarizing Marx's *Economic and Philosophic Manuscripts of 1844,* as they are now called.

26. Gaddis shows his contempt for Skinner's "infantile ideas" (485) by dividing his name between the sleazy film producer B. F. Leva—whose initials Gibbs spells out (582)—and the philandering book salesman Skinner, subject of an obscene limerick (677).

27. F. H. Knight, *The Ethics of Competition* (1935), quoted in Brown, *Life Against Death,* 238.

28. Wiener, *Human Use,* 20–21.

Chapter Five

1. L. J. Rather, *The Dream of Self-Destruction: Wagner's "Ring" and the Modern World* (Baton Rouge: Louisiana State University Press, 1979), 105.

2. T. S. Eliot, "Tradition and the Individual Talent," *Selected Prose,* 38.

3. Bob Minkoff, "Is Valhalla Burning?" *Cornell Daily Sun,* 24 October 1975, 4, 12; and Steven Weisenburger, "Contra Naturam?: Usury in William Gaddis's *J R,"* *Genre* 13 (Spring 1980):95–100.

4. Gaddis's references to *The Rhinegold* are taken from the synopsis in Gustave Kobbé's *The Complete Opera Book,* rev. ed. (New York: Putnam's, 1935), 149–52.

5. Quoted in Rather, *Dream,* 175. The poet is Goethe: see *Faust,* 11. 6057 ff.

6. George Bernard Shaw, *The Perfect Wagnerite: A Commentary on "The Niblung's Ring,"* 4th ed. (1923; reprint New York: Dover, 1967), 10, xvii. The quotations from Shaw that follow are from pp. 11–25.

7. All translations from *The Ring* are from Andrew Porter's *The Ring of the Nibelung* (New York: Norton, 1976). I follow Porter's English versions of Wagner's proper names except for Valhalla, which I prefer over his Walhall.

8. Deryck Cooke, *I Saw the World End: A Study of Wagner's "Ring"* (New York: Oxford University Press, 1976), 159.

9. George G. Windell, "Hitler, National Socialism, and Richard Wagner," in *Penetrating Wagner's "Ring": An Anthology*, ed. John Louis DiGaetani (Rutherford, N.J.: Fairleigh Dickinson University Press, 1978), 225.

10. William Gaddis, "J. R. or the Boy Inside," *Dutton Review* 1 (1970):25, 67; cf. *J R* 18, 43.

11. Amy is unaware that Gibbs and her older brother Freddie attended boarding school in Connecticut together: see 498, 618. (In *Carpenter's Gothic*, Liz is likewise unaware that her younger brother and McCandless's son Jack attended school together.)

12. Cooke, *I Saw the World*, 156.

13. H. R. Ellis Davidson, *Gods and Myths of Northern Europe* (Baltimore: Penguin, 1964), 115, 116 n. 1.

14. Other references during this brief scene (352–53) suggest that Stella has a sex life as active and perverse as Freya's: "Loki accused her of taking all the gods and elves for lovers, while the giantess Hyndla taunted her with roaming out at night like a she-goat among the bucks" (ibid., 115). Stella's lover lipsticks a design on her body that looks "like a cat with one large eye" (353), a mythologically relevant reminder that "Freyja's chariot is drawn, not by goats, rams or bulls, but by cats" (Cooke, *I Saw the World*, 155). Freia/Freya/Freyja are all related to the modern German verb *freien* (to woo, to marry), the subject of a quip in *The Recognitions* (195).

15. Ernest Newman, *Wagner as Man and Artist*, 2nd ed. (New York: Knopf, 1924), 349. Stella owns a copy of this book (146, 149), which is the source for the Wagneriana in Amy and Bast's conversation (111–16).

16. George Steiner, "Crossed Lines," *New Yorker*, 26 January 1976, 109.

17. Lionel Trilling, "Introduction," *Bouvard and Pécuchet* by Gustave Flaubert, trans. T. W. Earp and G. W. Stonier (Norfolk, Conn.: New Directions, 1954), v–vii.

18. Shaw, *The Perfect Wagnerite*, 9.

19. This famous line is quoted twice in *The Recognitions* (290, 559), both times with ironic implications.

20. Richard Ellmann, *Oscar Wilde* (New York: Knopf, 1988), 205. The text of Wilde's lecture can be found in *The Annotated Oscar Wilde*, ed. H. Montgomery Hyde (New York: Clarkson N. Potter, 1982), 379–82.

21. In Gaddis's version, "Saint Fiacre" is St. Vith, "Blaufinger" is probably General Hasso von Manteuffel, and "General Box" perhaps General R. W. Hasbrouck. Coincidentally, several accounts of the Ardennes offensive (a.k.a. the Battle of the Bulge) mention a Major Percy Schramm, a German historian who kept Hitler's diary on the offensive.

22. Conrad's *Lord Jim* (1900) also shares this theme and may be alluded to in *J R:* compare Gibbs's description of his book as "sort of a social history of mechanization and the arts, the destructive element" (244) with the trader Stein on the difficulty of maintaining an ideal in a hostile world: "The way is to the destructive element submit yourself, and with the exertions of your

hands and feet in the water make the deep, deep sea keep you up. So if you ask me—how to be? [. . .] I will tell you! [. . .] In the destructive element immerse" (chap. 20).

23. G. S. Kirk and J. E. Raven, *The Presocratic Philosophers* (Cambridge: Cambridge University Press, 1960), 336–38, Gaddis's probable source as the many parallels in diction suggest. The fullest treatment of Gaddis's use of Empedocles is Stephen Matanle's "Love and Strife in *J R*," in Kuehl and Moore, *In Recognition,* 106–18.

24. Shorn of its curlicues, the Greek phrase on p. 20 reads "FROM EACH ACCORD . . . "—from Marx's famous formulation in *Critique of the Gotha Program* (1875): "From each according to his abilities, to each according to his needs."

25. Lloyd Grove, "Harnessing the Power of Babble," *Washington Post,* 23 August 1985, B10.

26. Edmund Wilson, *The Wound and the Bow* (Cambridge, Mass.: Houghton Mifflin, 1941), 294.

Chapter Six

1. *Bard College Bulletin,* November 1984. Gaddis originally wrote two additional sentences: "Keeping the questions open, as I did at Bard, is a difficult way to teach; it's not like teaching mathematics. This puts a great deal of responsibility directly on the teacher's shoulders."

2. *Carpenter's Gothic* (1985; reprint, New York: Penguin, 1986), 130, 136, 191, 193, 240; hereafter cited in the text. This paperback edition contains a few corrections, adjusts the paragraphing on pp. 1 and 25, and restores a line accidentally dropped from the first edition.

3. McCandless is quoting reporter Dena Kleiman's article on Mel and Norma Gabler entitled "Influential Couple Scrutinize Books for 'Anti-Americanism,'" *New York Times,* 14 July 1981, C4.

4. Grove, "Harnessing the Power," B10.

5. The only anachronism in the novel's time scheme is the headline Liz notes on p. 28, which appeared on the front page of the *New York Times,* 25 July 1980.

6. Alexander Theroux, *Darconville's Cat* (Garden City, N.Y.: Doubleday, 1981), 73.

7. Fiedler, *Love and Death,* 131.

8. Ibid., 133.

9. *The Complete Works of Nathanael West* (New York: Farrar, Straus, 1957), 366.

10. Ozick, rev. of *Carpenter's Gothic,* 18. Cf. Robinson Jeffers's use of organic decay to describe America's decline in his poem "Shine, Perishing Republic" (1924), which Gaddis read while working on *Carpenter's Gothic*. He briefly considered using a phrase from this poem, "thickening to empire," as

the title for his third novel. (All the alternate titles I mention come from a conversation we had in August 1984.)

11. Frederick Busch, "A Bleak Vision of Gothic America," *Chicago Tribune,* 14 July 1985, "Bookworld," 28.

12. See Roy R. Male's *Enter, Mysterious Stranger: American Cloistral Fiction* (Norman: University of Oklahoma Press, 1979).

13. Michael Herr, *Dispatches* (New York: Knopf, 1977), 26.

14. The statistics are Gaddis's: see "The Rush for Second Place," 37.

15. Richard Poirier, review of *Gravity's Rainbow* by Thomas Pynchon, *Saturday Review of the Arts* 1 (3 March 1973):59.

16. Al J. Sperone, "Mr. Gaddis Builds His Dream House," *Village Voice,* 13 August 1985, 43.

17. I am indebted to Sarah E. Lauzen's witty and informative "Notes on Metafiction: Every Essay Has a Title," in *Postmodern Fiction: A Bio-Bibliographical Guide,* ed. Larry McCaffery (Westport, Conn.: Greenwood Press, 1986), 93–116. See also her essay on Gaddis in the same volume (374–77).

18. In "Tradition and the Individual Talent," Eliot writes, "Poetry is not a turning loose of emotion, but an escape from emotion; it is not the expression of personality, but an escape from personality. But, of course, only those who have personality and emotions know what it means to want to escape from these things" (*Selected Prose,* 43).

19. James Perrin Warren puts it differently: "The names record the attitudes of the namers: Billy needs a sister locked in the childhood he has never escaped; Paul needs a secretary; McCandless needs an adulteress; and Elizabeth needs an Elizabeth" (review of *Carpenter's Gothic, Southern Humanities Review* 21 [Spring 1987]:192).

20. Richard Toney, review of *Carpenter's Gothic, San Francisco Review of Books,* Fall/Winter 1985, 8. I should point out that this review and his earlier one in the same journal on *J R* (February 1976, 12–13) are otherwise quite insightful.

21. Johan Thielemans, "Intricacies of Plot: Some Preliminary Remarks to William Gaddis's *Carpenter's Gothic,*" in *Studies in Honour of René Derolez,* ed. A. M. Simon-Vandenbergen (Ghent: Seminarie voor Engelse en Oud-Germaanse Taalkunde, 1987), 617.

Chapter Seven

1. William Carlos Williams, *In the American Grain* (1925; reprint, New York: New Directions, 1956), 109.

2. R. W. B. Lewis, afterword to *The Confidence-Man* by Herman Melville (New York: New American Library, 1964), 263.

3. John Brooks, "Fiction of the Managerial Class," *New York Times Book Review,* 8 April 1984, 36. See also Emily Stripes Watts's *The Businessman in American Literature* (Athens: University of Georgia Press, 1982), whose half-dozen references to *J R* are similarly unsympathetic.

4. Henry Nash Smith, "The Search for a Capitalist Hero" (1964), as quoted in Watts, ibid., 3.

5. Alicia Metcalf Miller, review of *J R*, *Cleveland Plain-Dealer*, 9 November 1975, 5:14.

6. The "attractive girl with the Boston voice" who recommends benny (*R* 631, 640) took her lines from Burroughs's Mary (*Junky* [1953; reprint, New York: Penguin, 1977], 14), who was based on a six-foot redhead named Vicki Russell—not from Boston but, like Liz, from Grosse Pointe.

7. Markson writes: "There is no question in my mind that *The Recognitions* is the monumental American novel of the century. And, having read it twice when it came out, and then again perhaps five years later, I'd find it a miracle if I *hadn't* been influenced. Certainly in writing my novel *Going Down*, not only with a good deal of the intellectual materials I felt licensed to use, but also in the way I used them, I found Gaddis inescapable. I mean quite literally in what I allowed my central character to 'know,' for instance. But probably 'inescapable' is the wrong word, since I believed the influence to be liberating more than anything else" (letter to me dated 11 January 1988).

8. Joseph McElroy, "Neural Neighborhoods and Other Concrete Abstracts," *TriQuarterly* 34 (Fall 1975):205.

9. Robert R. Harris, "A Talk with Don DeLillo," *New York Times Book Review*, 10 October 1982, 26. See also Tom LeClair's *In the Loop: Don DeLillo and the Systems Novel* (Urbana: University of Illinois Press, 1987), which contains numerous references to Gaddis.

10. Steven Moore, "'Parallel, Not Series': Thomas Pynchon and William Gaddis," *Pynchon Notes* 11 (February 1983):6–26.

11. Thomas Moore, *The Style of Connectedness: "Gravity's Rainbow" and Thomas Pynchon* (Columbia: University of Missouri Press, 1987), 20–21.

12. Bradford Morrow, "An Interview with Joseph McElroy," *Conjunctions* 10 (May 1987):151.

13. See chap. 1, n. 35 above; hereafter cited in the text. The new novel will be called *The Last Act* and "will progress largely through lawsuits, legal opinions, directly or indirectly interweaving a host of characters," according to Gaddis's editor; see "World Rights to Gaddis's Next Novel Bought by S & S," *Publishers Weekly*, 19 February 1988, 43.

14. D. W. Jefferson, "*Tristram Shandy* and the Tradition of Learned Wit," in Laurence Sterne's *Tristram Shandy*, ed. Howard Anderson (New York: Norton, 1980), 506. The preceding quotation from *Tristram Shandy* appears on p. 231 of this edition.

15. Hills, "Don't Everybody," 100. When two friends and I visited Gaddis in May 1986, we found him researching torts involving negligence and admiring the "elegance" of someone's opinion. He was looking forward to the arrival of eighty volumes of *American Jurisprudence* a legal admirer was sending him, though he would have preferred, he said, the *Corpus Juris Civilis*.

Selected Bibliography

PRIMARY SOURCES

Books

Carpenter's Gothic. New York: Viking, 1985; paperback edition with corrections, New York: Penguin, 1986.
J R. New York: Alfred A. Knopf, 1975; paperback edition with corrections, New York: Penguin, 1985.
The Recognitions. New York: Harcourt, Brace, 1955; paperback edition with corrections, New York: Penguin, 1985.

Magazine Contributions

"An Instinct for the Dangerous Wife" (review of *More Die of Hearbreak* by Saul Bellow). *New York Times Book Review,* 24 May 1987, 1, 16.
"In the Zone." *New York Times,* 13 March 1978, 21.
"J. R. or the Boy Inside." *Dutton Review* 1 (1970):5–68.
"Les Chemin des Anes." *New World Writing* 1 (April 1952):210–22.
"Nobody Grew but the Business," *Harper's,* June 1975, 47–54, 59–66.
"The Rush for Second Place." *Harper's,* April 1981, 31–39.
"'Stop Player. Joke No. 4.'" *Atlantic Monthly,* July 1951, 92–93.
"Szyrk v. Village of Tatamount et al." *New Yorker,* 12 October 1987, 44–50.
"Trickle-Up Economics: J R Goes to Washington." *New York Times Book Review,* 25 October 1987, 29.
"Untitled Fragment from Another Damned, Thick, Square Book." *Antæus* 13/14 (Spring/Summer 1974):98–105.

Interviews

Abádi-Nagy, Zoltán. "The Art of Fiction CI: William Gaddis." *Paris Review* 105 (Winter 1987):54–89.
Berkley, Miriam. "PW Interviews: William Gaddis." *Publishers Weekly,* 12 July 1985, 56–57.
Bradbury, Malcolm. *Writers in Conversation 13: William Gaddis.* London: Institute of Contemporary Arts, 1986. Videocassette distributed by the Rowland Collection, Northbrook, Ill.
Friedman, Stanley P. "Five Novelists at Work: A Grapeshot Interview." *Book World,* 10 March 1968, 10.
Grove, Lloyd. "Harnessing the Power of Babble: The Rich, Comic, Talkative Novels of William Gaddis." *Washington Post,* 23 August 1985, "Style," B1, B10.

Kuehl, John, and Steven Moore. "An Interview with William Gaddis." *Review of Contemporary Fiction* 2, no. 2 (Summer 1982):4–6.

LeClair, Thomas. "Missing Writers." *Horizon,* October 1981, 48–52.

Logan, Marie-Rose, and Tomasz Mirkowicz. "'Kto do utworu przychodzi z niczym . . . ': Z Williamem Gaddisem rozmawiają" ("If You Bring Nothing to a Work . . . ": An Interview with William Gaddis). *Literatura na Świecie* 1/150 (1984):178–89. In Polish.

SECONDARY SOURCES

Books and Symposia

Kuehl, John, and Steven Moore, eds. *In Recognition of William Gaddis.* Syracuse: Syracuse University Press, 1984. Contains a biographical introduction, thirteen essays (six previously unpublished), and the most extensive bibliography to date.

Moore, Steven. *A Reader's Guide to William Gaddis's "The Recognitions."* Lincoln: University of Nebraska Press, 1982. An introduction and set of annotations to the first novel.

Review of Contemporary Fiction. William Gaddis / Nicholas Mosley Number. 2, no. 2 (Summer 1982). Contains the Kuehl/Moore interview, seven essays, and a bibliography.

Parts of Books and Articles

This list does not include separate essays published in the two symposia above, both of which contain fuller bibliographies than the selective list that follows.

Auchincloss, Louis. "Recognizing Gaddis." *New York Times Magazine,* 15 November 1987, 36, 38, 41, 54, 58. Useful for new biographical material.

Comnes, Gregory. "A Patchwork of Conceits: Perspective and Perception in *Carpenter's Gothic." Critique* 30, no. 1 (1988):13–26. An insightful discussion of the ways Gaddis's third novel differs from his two earlier ones.

Green, Jack. "fire the bastards!" (parts 1–3). *newspaper* 12–14 (24 February, 25 August, 10 November 1962):1–76. A lively history of *The Recognitions's* critical reception 1955–62.

Karl, Frederick R. *American Fictions 1940–1980.* New York: Harper & Row, 1983. The principal sections on Gaddis are reprinted in Kuehl and Moore's *In Recognition,* but Gaddis is mentioned throughout as a touchstone for contemporary American fiction. For a harsh critique of Karl's book, however, with special reference to his reading of *J R,* see Bruce Bawer's "The Novel in the Academy," *New Criterion,* May 1984, 20–30.

Koenig, Peter William. "Recognizing Gaddis' *Recognitions." Contemporary Lit-*

erature 16 (Winter 1975):61–72. Valuable for its quotations from Gaddis's manuscript notes.

LaCapra, Dominick. "Singed Phoenix and Gift of Tongues: William Gaddis's *The Recognitions.*" *Diacritics* 16, no. 4 (Winter 1986):33–47. Sees the novel "as the epitome of Mikhail Bakhtin's notion of the significant novel as the polyphonic orchestration of the heterogeneous, fragmentary, often chaotic, at times cacophonous discourses of the times into a serio-comic, provocatively ambivalent *agon* or carnival of contending 'voices' and dissonant possibilities in society and culture."

LeClair, Thomas. "William Gaddis, *J R,* & the Art of Excess." *Modern Fiction Studies* 27 (Winter 1981–82):587–600. A brilliant examination of the excessive nature of Gaddis's work and the waste motif in his second novel.

Lewicki, Zbigniew. *The Bang and the Whimper: Apocalypse and Entropy in American Literature.* Westport, Conn.: Greenwood Press, 1984, 103–8. On *J R*'s "irreversible process of entropic decay and disintegration of people, objects, and information."

Moore, Steven. "Chronological Difficulties in the Novels of William Gaddis." *Critique* 22, no. 1 (1980):79–91. An attempt to establish the time schemes of the first two novels, but too literal-minded to accommodate Gaddis's flexible temporal structures.

Safer, Elaine B. "The Allusive Mode, the Absurd and Black Humor in William Gaddis's *The Recognitions.*" *Studies in American Humor* n. s. 1 (October 1982):103–18. Examines Gaddis's ironic use of literary allusion and the absurdist vision that results.

Tanner, Tony. *City of Words: American Fiction 1950–1970.* New York: Harper & Row, 1971, 393–400. A valuable early study of the aesthetic dimensions of *The Recognitions,* especially imitation vs. invention and art as a means of "recognizing" reality.

Thielemans, Johan. "Gaddis and the Novel of Entropy." *TREMA* [Travaux et Recherches sur le Monde Anglophone] 2 (1977):97–107. An excellent study of communication in *J R.*

———. "Intricacies of Plot: Some Preliminary Remarks to William Gaddis's *Carpenter's Gothic.*" In *Studies in Honour of René Derolez.* ed. A. M. Simon-Vandenbergen. Ghent: Seminarie voor Engelse en Oud-Germaanse Taalkunde R.U.G., 1987, 612–21. The first essay-length attempt to unravel the plot of Gaddis's third novel.

Weisenburger, Steven. "Contra Naturam?: Usury in William Gaddis's *J R.*" *Genre* 13 (Spring 1980):93–109; reprinted in *Money Talks: Language and Lucre in American Fiction,* ed. Roy R. Male. Norman: University of Oklahoma Press, 1981. An instructive look at some of the fields of reference operative in *J R,* especially good on Wagner.

Index